# Violence
# &
# the Bible

## FOR NORMAL PEOPLE

A Guide to
Biblical Texts of Terror

*Caroline Blyth*

THE BIBLE
FOR NORMAL PEOPLE

Library of Congress Control Number: 2025900859

ISBN: 978-1-964423-24-1 (Paperback)
ISBN: 978-1-964423-25-8 (Hardcover)
ISBN: 978-1-964423-26-5 (eBook)

Cover design: Jacqueline Hunt

*To Em, my partner in crime*

# Table of Contents

# Infomercial

Hi, I'm Caroline. I'm a biblical scholar who hails from Scotland, and I have spent most of my academic career wrestling with portrayals of violence in the Bible. My aim in this book is to travel with you as we explore some of these texts together and consider their ongoing legacy. I hope you find the journey as fascinating as I do.

Before we begin, let me tell you a secret. I've been a bit obsessed with violence and crime since a very early age. As a child, I was hooked on Nancy Drew novels, and I harbored dreams of becoming a kick-ass sleuth, just like Nancy. Once I reached my teens, I graduated to the murder mysteries of Agatha Christie, P. D. James, and Arthur Conan Doyle. I may not have realized it at the time, but I was giving myself the perfect education for a career as a scholar of biblical violence.[1]

The Bible is a violent book, of that there is no doubt.[2] There are stories of murder, warfare, genocide, execution, enslavement, mutilation,

---

1 My plans to pursue a career in sleuthing never really panned out, so biblical scholarship seemed like a decent second choice.

2 Throughout this book, I use the term "Bible" as shorthand for the Tanakh (Jewish sacred scripture) and the Christian New Testament. The Tanakh contains the same biblical books that were later included in the Protestant Old Testament, albeit in a different order. Biblical scholars often use the term "Hebrew Bible" rather than "Tanakh," but I prefer the latter as it serves as a useful acronym (TaNaKh) for the three main sections in this sacred collection of texts: Torah (teachings: Genesis–Deuteronomy), Nevi'im (prophets:

dismemberment, rape, intimate partner violence, and human sacrifice. Woven through many of these "texts of terror"[3] are the threads of injustice, intolerance, and the abuse of power, all of which ignite violence and keep it burning brightly. In others, we are shown how emotions such as fear, anger, jealousy, and shame can inspire violent actions, often with lethal effect. All in all, the violence depicted in the pages of the Bible comes in various shapes and sizes, from divine retribution executed on a cosmic scale to individual acts of harm committed by one person against another.

Now, for many readers, this abundance of biblical violence won't come as a surprise. After all, some of the most well-known stories in the Bible depict seriously brutal events: the cataclysmic flood (Genesis 6–9); the destruction of Sodom and Gomorrah (Genesis 19); the Egyptian plagues (Exodus 7–12); the conquest of Canaan (Joshua 6–11); David's slaying of Goliath (1 Samuel 17); the passion and crucifixion of Jesus (Matthew 27; Mark 15; Luke 22–23; John 19); and, last but by no means least, the mother of all cosmic battles in the book of Revelation.

I've always wondered why *so many* violent stories wound up in the Bible in the first place: what was it about these terrifying tales that inspired the Bible's authors and editors to record them and share them? Why did they captivate ancient audiences and inspire early Jewish and Christian communities to count them as part of their sacred scripture?

---

Joshua, Judges, 1 and 2 Samuel, 1 and 2 Kings, Isaiah, Jeremiah, Ezekiel, and the book of the twelve, i.e. Hosea–Malachi), and Ketuvim (writings: Psalms, Proverbs, Job, Song of Solomon, Ruth, Lamentations, Ecclesiastes, Esther, Daniel, Ezra, Nehemiah, and 1 and 2 Chronicles). I also prefer using the term "Tanakh" rather than "Old Testament" because "Old" suggests the problematic idea that Jewish scriptures are outdated and obsolete or that they are deficient without the addition of the Christian New Testament.

3 I borrow the term "texts of terror" from biblical scholar Phyllis Trible and her seminal work *Texts of Terror: Literary-Feminist Readings of Biblical Narratives,* 40th anniversary ed. (Minneapolis: Fortress, 2022) Originally published in 1984, this book was groundbreaking in its analysis of gender-based violence in the Bible, and it has been an inspiration for me throughout my own studies.

Perhaps we can find an answer to these questions if we consider the enduring and widespread popularity of violent narratives that exist beyond the pages of the Bible. Tales of murder, brutality, and crime have intrigued the public for millennia, and many societies throughout history have recounted infamously bloody acts of violence in the popular culture of the day, including in myths and legends, song ballads, novels, poems, plays, broadsheets, and even puppet shows. Today, crime novels remain one of the best-selling literary genres, and crime dramas and true crime documentaries are almost guaranteed to generate high audience figures.

So what can possibly explain this ongoing fascination with violence? One possible theory is that violent stories are popular because they give audiences the chance to think about violence "from a safer distance." In other words, narratives depicting violence (whether real or fictional) let us explore the realities of violence without having to experience them ourselves. Or, if we *have* been victimized by violence, these narratives may give us an outlet for safely revisiting our experiences or processing our trauma. They shine a light on issues that make many of us anxious or uneasy—danger, loss, injury, injustice, betrayal, pain, and death. They offer us ways to contemplate how violence could impact (or has impacted) us, as well as our families and communities. They allow us to tentatively untangle the emotional causes and consequences of violence so that we can better understand why people act violently and how violence affects their victims. These stories let us mull over knotty spiritual and philosophical questions about good and evil. And they may also serve as cautionary tales, which remind us to keep ourselves safe, to stop and think before we act violently ourselves, and to never forget the lasting imprint that violence can leave on us all.

If we apply this theory about the function of violent stories to the stories of violence in the Bible, we might get a clue about why these texts were so meaningful for their ancient audiences. We might also discover why they continue to have meaning for audiences today. Like their contemporary counterparts, biblical texts of terror invite us to think about the repercussions and legacies of violence "from a safer distance." They ask us to recognize the significance of violence for the individuals and communities inhabiting the biblical world. More than that, though, violent biblical texts challenge us to see the legacy they've left in our *own* lives and communities. As I'll show you in the following chapters, this legacy packs a punch (pardon the pun), and it's enduring. Depictions of biblical violence are like pebbles thrown into a pond— they send out ripple after ripple across time and space. And for that reason alone, they are worth exploring further.

So let's get ready to start our journey into the world of biblical violence. Whatever has inspired you to travel with me as you read this book, be assured that you're in safe hands. I'm a pretty good guide, I won't get us lost, and although the going might get a bit tough at times, I promise I'll bring you home safely.

# CHAPTER ONE

# Violence in the Bible from 30,000 Feet

This chapter will prepare us for our journey through the Bible's texts of terror. I'll begin by offering a definition of the term "violence," and I'll also outline the different categories of violence we encounter in the Jewish Tanakh and the Christian New Testament. Then, I'll explain the key themes I'll be using throughout the book to unpack and investigate biblical violence. Lastly, I'll lay out a roadmap of where the rest of the book will take us—our various stops along the way before we get to our final destination.

## Defining Violence

Dictionary definitions of "violence" often present it as something physical—a forceful action or behavior inflicted on someone or something. The Merriam-Webster dictionary, for example, defines violence first and foremost as "the use of physical force so as to injure, abuse, damage, or destroy."[1] Yet "violence" can mean far more than an act of physical aggression: there can be violence in hurtful words and images;

---

1 Merriam-Webster Dictionary, "violence," https://thebiblefornormalpeople. com/classes/.

in threats, bullying, and intimidation; in laws and institutions that perpetuate injustice; and in beliefs and ideologies that promote intolerance and hatred.[2] Similarly, the effects of violence are far more diverse than physical injury alone. Violence can have an intense emotional impact on its victims, turning their world upside down and knocking the feet from under them.

In light of all this, I believe it's helpful to think of "violence" as an umbrella term, which includes a range of behaviors, vocabularies, and beliefs that can diminish or even extinguish a person's ability to flourish or survive. To help you navigate your way around this umbrella, I've organized the violence we'll be discussing throughout this book into four separate categories: physical violence, gender-based violence, the violence of language, and structural violence. As you'll see, these categories do overlap with each other at times, but I think they can still help us recognize the diverse (and sometimes hidden) ways that violence can occur. I'll go through each of them in turn, explaining what they entail, and I'll also offer some examples of where we can find these forms of violence in the biblical texts.

## Killing, Warring, Smiting: Physical Violence

Physical violence involves the use of force against a person or persons that is likely to cause them injury, harm, trauma, or even death. It can be deemed unlawful in some cases (e.g. assaults, armed robberies, murders, kidnappings) and lawful in others (e.g. state-sanctioned executions and military action). Physical violence also encompasses a spectrum of behaviors that vary in terms of their severity and duration, from a one-off slap on the face all the way to a prolonged onslaught of genocidal warfare.

---

2 I'm focusing here on violence perpetrated by and against human beings, but I believe that much of what I say also applies to violence against other-than-human creatures. There are certainly plenty of examples of such violence in the biblical texts, but unfortunately, this book isn't big enough for me to draw our feathered, finned, and furry friends into the conversation.

There's a lot of physical violence depicted in the texts of the Tanakh and New Testament, including murders, wars, physical assaults, and executions. Only four chapters into the first book of the Tanakh, Adam and Eve's son Cain murders his younger brother Abel in a fit of sibling rivalry (Genesis 4:8). A mere fifteen verses later, Cain's great-great-great-grandson Lamech boasts that he's killed a man for hitting him (Genesis 4:23). This idea that violence begets violence crops up again in other biblical texts, and it may reflect how violence was understood by these ancient writers. Cain's homicidal violence seems to act like a catalyst that inspires others to follow his lead, and murder becomes an all-too-common means of dealing with a rival, exacting revenge, or escaping a tricky situation. And as I'll explore further in Chapter 2, not all biblical murders are viewed in a negative light—a lot depends on *who* the murderer is and *why* they commit the murder.

Lethal violence of another kind also makes an appearance in the Tanakh and New Testament, although this time, it's perfectly legit (according to these texts, at least). Capital punishment is instituted in the legal systems operating in biblical Israel and first-century Palestine. In the law codes of the Tanakh (found in Exodus–Deuteronomy), certain misdemeanors (including murder, sorcery, adultery, incest, and giving your parents grief) were punishable with death by stoning or, less often, by burning. And under Roman imperial rule, crucifixion was used as a form of capital punishment for certain wrongdoers, such as rebellious enslaved people[3] and enemies of the state. I'll come back to the topic of Jesus's crucifixion in Chapter 6.

Another form of "legitimate" physical violence is the violence of warfare, and this also makes a regular appearance in the biblical texts. In the Tanakh, Israelite history is liberally peppered with stories of military activity, which recount both Israel's victories and its defeats.

---

3 I've chosen to use the term "enslaved people" rather than "slaves" throughout this book in recognition that enslavement is not a defining feature of a person's identity; rather, it's a condition imposed on them involuntarily by someone more powerful than them. For the same reason, I use "enslaver" rather than "slave owner" and "enslavement" rather than "slavery."

What's particularly interesting about these stories is that they regularly center God in the midst of the battle. This theme recurs in the New Testament book of Revelation, where the deity leads a heavenly army against the forces of evil. In Chapter 3, I'll discuss the imagery used in the Tanakh and New Testament to portray God as a warrior who orchestrates battles and even fights alongside the troops to ensure their victory.

Of course, war is not the only form of physical violence that God is depicted as enacting in the biblical texts. As I'll demonstrate in Chapter 3, the deity regularly strikes, smites, and annihilates those who are a source of divine displeasure. In various texts, God kills individuals, attempts to kill them, or inflicts them with grievous bodily harm. At other times, God's violent inclinations are meted out against entire communities, cities, nations, and even creation in its entirety. God also delegates various divine creatures to carry out the dirty work of enacting physical violence: angels of death, evil spirits, and other heavenly henchmen strike down individuals and wipe out thousands—including men, women, and children—at the deity's behest.

These depictions of a violent deity sit shoulder-to-shoulder in the Tanakh and New Testament with many other texts that speak of God's limitless love and eternal justice. For some readers, this may seem confounding and even disturbing—how can a god who is "merciful and gracious, slow to anger, and abounding in steadfast love and faithfulness" (Exodus 34:6) also be a god[4] of war, murder, and destruction? How can a just and righteous god be complicit in the killing of children? I'll let you into a secret: there are no easy answers to these

---

4 For purely grammatical reasons, I prefer lowercase "god" when I'm using the word as a common noun meaning "deity" or "divine being." "God" with a capital letter is a proper name, so it doesn't really work in phrases that describe God's biblical persona (such as "god of Israel" or "god of war"). In other words, "God is the god of Israel" has the same grammatical sense as "Dean is the dean of our local college."

questions, but I'll work through some of the implications they have for Bible readers during my discussion of divine violence in Chapter 3.[5]

Before we move on from divine violence, there's another type of physical violence that the biblical God is involved in (or at least implicated in), and that is child sacrifice. Now, there is some debate among biblical scholars about how the ancient writers understood the deity's complicity in this practice. In a number of texts, the act of sacrificing children to a god is attributed to "the nations"—in other words, anyone *but* Israel (e.g. Deuteronomy 12:29–31)—and it's made perfectly clear that this ritual is abhorrent and sinful. At the same time, though, other texts (e.g. Judges 11:29–40) do suggest that child sacrifice may have been a bona fide method of appeasing, obeying, or petitioning Israel's god. Rest assured, I'll tease this out further in Chapter 6, and I'll also reflect on the theological understanding of Jesus's crucifixion as a form of sacrifice.

There are many other types of physical violence depicted in the Bible, including beatings, bashings, maulings, muggings, and knifings. There's even a night-long wrestling match. I don't have the space to mention them all here, but by now, I hope you have a sense of the range and extent of the physical violence that's depicted in the biblical texts. And in some of the chapters that follow, I'll unpack the meanings that these violent tales might have had for the ancient writers and their audiences, as well as the meanings that they can offer us today as we reflect on physical violence in our own communities and contexts.

## Power and Control: Gender-Based Violence

"Gender-based violence" is another umbrella term used to capture a range of violent behaviors.[6] Essentially, gender-based violence can be defined as violence perpetrated against a person *because of* their gender.

---

5 Be forewarned, I'm *not* a theologian, but I am an expert in rooting out why violent characters in texts are depicted the way they are.

6 In other words, it's an umbrella underneath a bigger umbrella.

This violence takes many forms, including sexual violence, intimate partner violence, and coercive control.[7]

At its heart, gender-based violence is caused by a power imbalance, where people of one gender have better access to power than people of a different gender. We see this play out particularly in patriarchal societies, where men tend to be given access to a disproportionate share of social, economic, religious, and political power. Even in supposedly egalitarian nations today (which, let's be honest, are still pretty patriarchal), men enjoy certain privileges simply by virtue of being men; they generally earn more than women,[8] and they're also more likely than women to be granted positions of authority and leadership in their families, communities, and places of work, as well as the institutions they belong to.[9] And if that weren't enough, men and boys in patriarchal societies are often taught from an early age that they're *entitled* to this unequal share of power purely because of their gender.

---

7 I'll offer definitions of these terms in Chapters 3 and 4.

8 The gender pay-gap is still very real; globally, women's wages are on average 30% less than men's. But when broken down country by country, other markers of identity (particularly ethnicity) intersect with gender to make the disparity even greater for some women. To take the United States as an example, for every dollar paid to non-Hispanic white men, non-Hispanic white women are paid 81 cents, Black women are paid 66 cents, Native Hawaiian and Pacific Island women are paid 61 cents, First Nations women are paid 55 cents, and Latina women are paid 52 cents. You can find out more in the World Economic Forum's "Global Gender Gap Report 2023," https://www.weforum.org/publications/global-gender-gap-report-2023/in-full/benchmarking-gender-gaps-2023/, and at AAUW, "The Simple Truth About the Gender Pay Gap," https://www.aauw.org/resources/research/simple-truth/.

9 I've heard many (annoying) people dispute this claim by pointing out that women today *can* attain power and authority, and they'll usually refer to national leaders like Nicola Sturgeon, Jacinda Ardern, Julia Gillard, and Angela Merkel to back up their argument. Now, I agree, it isn't impossible for women to achieve positions of authority; but, statistically, it's far, far rarer for them to do so and a great deal harder, too. Women who achieve political power are like black swans—the exceptions that prove the rule.

Now, there are many men who use their power and privilege to foster justice and equality within their own communities and further afield, too. But there are also men who feel entitled to their power, so they choose to hold onto it (or even increase it) by dominating and controlling those who have less power than them. This domination and control can take many different forms, including gender-based violence.

As many of you will be aware, perpetrators of gender-based violence are most commonly men, while women and girls are more likely to be victims. That being said, it is *not* the case that men and boys *can't* be victims of such violence or that women *can't* be perpetrators. They can, and they are. But statistically, most victims of gender-based violence are women and girls,[10] and most perpetrators are men. And I believe that this is directly related to the imbalance of power between men and women that remains a global phenomenon, even today. In other words, it's a man's world, and women and girls pay the price.[11]

The relationship between gender-based violence and access to power is such an important point to keep in mind when we look at this form of violence in the biblical texts. In the patriarchal landscapes of the Bible, women were typically viewed as occupying a subordinate position to men in both the family and society; they had less legal, social, political, and religious power than men.[12] And this left them especially vulnerable to gender-based violence, which is illustrated all too clearly in the biblical texts.

---

10 And here, I include transgender women and girls, not least because they are *especially* vulnerable to gender-based violence.

11 I am aware that other aspects of a person's identity, besides their gender, can impact their access to power and render them even more vulnerable to gender-based violence. I'll talk about this shortly in the section on structural violence, as well as in Chapter 5.

12 Of course, there are exceptions, and a few biblical women seem to occupy positions of authority as leaders, prophets, and business owners. But to echo what I said in an earlier footnote, these powerful women are a rarity—the exceptions that prove the rule.

For example, sexual violence is a recurring theme throughout the Tanakh, and it is also alluded to in the New Testament book of Revelation. There are narratives depicting the rapes and threatened rapes of individual women, and there are multiple references to the captivity and rape of women and girls during warfare. Intimate partner violence is also portrayed, particularly in the so-called "marriage metaphor" that appears in the prophetic books of Ezekiel and Hosea. In this metaphorical depiction of God's anger at the covenant community, God takes the role of a cuckolded husband who coercively controls and emotionally abuses his[13] allegedly unfaithful "wife" (the people of Israel and Judah) by threatening to punish her with sexual and physical violence. I'll discuss a number of these texts of terror in Chapters 3 and 4, and I'll also illustrate how they echo the same damaging misperceptions about rape and intimate partner violence that we still hear so often today in the media and in public life.

Sexual enslavement is another form of biblical gender-based violence, and I'll talk about this practice in Chapter 5. Enslaved women were especially vulnerable to sexual abuse and harm; as the "property" of their enslavers, they had no power to control their own bodies or their sexuality. In biblical Israel, they were sometimes taken as "wives" by their male enslavers in order to be impregnated. Any child born of such a union was deemed the legitimate offspring of the woman's enslavers, rather than of the woman herself. The most well-known victim of this form of gender-based violence is the enslaved Egyptian woman Hagar, whom Sarai "gives" to her husband Abram after Sarai is unable to bear a child of her own (Genesis 16). This pattern is repeated again by Rachel and Leah, the wives of Abraham's grandson Jacob. Like Sarai, both women direct their husband to impregnate two enslaved women, Bilhah and Zilpah, in order to generate more sons (Genesis 30:1–13). These stories serve as a reminder that, in the biblical texts,

---

13 I tend not to use pronouns in reference to God, but when I discuss the marriage metaphor (here and in Chapter 3), I do use "he/him" as God is explicitly portrayed as a husband.

women were sometimes complicit in enacting gender-based violence against women and girls who were less powerful than them.

All in all, biblical women encounter many forms of gender-based violence due to their relative lack of power. But we can't forget that some biblical men are also vulnerable to this form of violence, especially when they experience episodes of powerlessness themselves. There are four biblical texts of terror where men are raped or threatened with rape (Genesis 19:1–11, 30–38; 39:6–20; Judges 19:22), and I'll talk about these in Chapters 4 and 5.

For some readers of this book, the sheer extent of biblical gender-based violence may come as a surprise. When I first started my PhD, a friend asked me what I was planning to write about. When I told her I was focusing on biblical rape narratives, she stared at me, aghast. "Rape? In the Bible? Are you sure?" Her response is understandable, though: biblical texts depicting gender-based violence don't tend to get included with any regularity in sermons, seminary classes, church lectionaries, or retellings of biblical stories in popular culture. Or if they do get a mention, the violence within them is often glossed over. As I'll discuss further in Chapters 3 and 4, biblical gender-based violence is a lot like gender-based violence in many societies today—it's all too often ignored, downplayed, excused, or denied.

## Sticks and Stones: The Violence of Language

If you're as old as me,[14] you might remember being told as a kid that sticks and stones might break your bones, but words can never hurt you. My mother would always say that to me whenever I started whining that my sister had called me a rude name (again). And throughout my life, I've often heard people trot out something similar: "They're only words—I didn't mean any harm," or "Oh, just ignore her. Her bark is worse than her bite."

---

14 I was born in the latter half of the 1900s—that makes me ancient, right?

Now, if push came to shove, I'm sure many of us would prefer to be "hit" by a harsh word rather than by a blunt instrument. But we ignore the violence of language at our peril. Language can be used to demean, threaten, oppress, or dehumanize an individual or group. Words and images become weaponized to bully people, discriminate against them, identify them as a threat, or even categorize them as being less deserving of a livable life. Any form of language (be it words, images, or ideas) can be as sharp as any knife and as penetrating as any arrow; it can cut its victims to the quick and pierce their hearts, leaving them with lasting wounds.

A number of texts in the Bible confirm that language can be a deadly weapon and the source of injustice and oppression. The words of the wicked are likened to a "deadly arrow" (Jeremiah 9:8 [MT 9:7]),[15] a "sharp razor" (Psalm 52:2), and a "deadly ambush" (Proverbs 12:5–6). Yet despite these warnings, there are violent words aplenty in the Bible, and they're not always coming forth from the mouths of the unrighteous. God is often portrayed as using violent language to keep the covenant community in check and to warn (i.e., threaten) them when they're misbehaving. We see this happen *a lot* in the Nevi'im (prophets) section of the Tanakh, where prophets such as Isaiah, Jeremiah, Ezekiel, and Amos pass on messages to the Israelites which they claim come directly from God. These guys[16] are experts at delivering outrageously menacing words on the deity's behalf—it's what they do best. They use violent language and imagery depicting all manner of horrors to grab their audiences' attention and make them realize the trouble they're in. I'll be talking about this in more depth in Chapter 3.

---

15 Sometimes, the verse numbers in English Bible translations are ever so slightly different to the verse numbers in the Tanakh, which follows the Hebrew manuscript known as the Masoretic Text (MT). So whenever this happens, I'll add the Hebrew chapter and verse numbers in brackets after the English ones.

16 Yes, I know there are female prophets mentioned in the Tanakh, but *they* don't feel the need to threaten everyone all the time.

Meanwhile, in the New Testament, Jesus follows in the prophets' footsteps by sometimes using explicitly violent language to capture people's attention. He may be remembered as a preacher who proclaimed a gospel of peace and love, but there are plenty of occasions when he doesn't mince his words. In the Gospels, he accuses his detractors of being "a brood of vipers," "snakes," "hypocrites," and "blind fools" (Matthew 15:7; 23:13–36). He tells some of his fellow Jews that their father is "the devil" (John 8:44). And as I'll discuss in Chapter 5, he also draws on the violent language of enslavement to illustrate some of his parables and sayings. Furthermore, in the book of Revelation, the risen Christ castigates a female prophet called Jezebel by threatening to throw her on a bed and "strike her children dead" (Revelation 2:20–23).

But Jesus isn't the only New Testament figure to resort to violent language: the apostle Paul gives him a run for his money. In a number of Paul's epistles (letters), he delivers biting words to those who don't accept God or the gospel of Jesus Christ: he threatens them with divine vengeance, warns them that he'll visit them with a "stick" (1 Corinthians 4:21), and even wishes that that those who "unsettle" Jesus followers would "castrate themselves" (Galatians 5:12). Yikes.

Now, some may still argue that these examples of violent language are far less dangerous than other forms of violence. Sticks and stones, right? No, not necessarily, because the violent words we see in the Bible rarely stay on the page—they leak out into the world, where they are translated into other forms of violence that can stigmatize, injure, and even kill. Cultural theorist Mieke Bal once said that "the Bible, of all books, is the most dangerous one, the one that has been endowed with the power to kill."[17] She wasn't suggesting that biblical texts *literally* commit acts of violence, or that the Bible is the *only* source of violence in the world; rather, her point was that the violent words and imagery included in the Bible have a long, long history of being used (or rather,

---

17 Mieke Bal, *On Story-Telling: Essays in Narratology,* ed. David Jobling (Sonoma, CA: Polebridge, 1981), 14.

misused) to justify or endorse violence. I'll return to this point in some of the following chapters.

## Hierarchies and Ladders: Structural Violence

Structural violence can be more difficult to define than the other forms of violence I've spoken about so far, and that's because it's not always caused by something we can see, like a weapon, a clenched fist, or angry words on a page. Instead, structural violence is caused by beliefs and attitudes that help to construct unjust social hierarchies.[18] Think of these hierarchies as being like a ladder, where the top rungs are reserved for the socially dominant group (the in-crowd, if you like) and the lowest rungs are for those who are labeled as undesirable, dangerous, or "polluting" in some sense. All too often, people's place on this ladder is determined by certain traits that they have. Now, these traits are usually value-neutral (or at least, they should be)—like skin color, ethnicity, gender identity, sexuality, religious faith, disability, or ancestry—but that doesn't stop them being used to determine where people "rightfully belong" on the ladder. Some traits are arbitrarily chosen as "proof" that people are inferior and that they deserve to be pushed down to a lower rung, where they have far less access to social, economic, political, and religious power (yes, we're back to power again). Meanwhile, other traits are held up as evidence of a person's superiority and as "proof" that they are entitled to their spot at the top of the ladder, where they can enjoy more power and privilege. In essence, then, the structural violence inherent to these hierarchies is the violence of injustice, where, for no logical reason, certain people are deprived of their rights and given restricted access to the resources they need to lead a livable life.

---

18 For my discussion throughout this section, I'm drawing heavily on Isabel Wilkerson's book *Caste: The Origins of Our Discontent* (New York: Random House, 2023). If you've not read *Caste*, I'd strongly recommend that you do— it's brilliant and powerful. You can also learn more about it, and about Isabel Wilkerson, in the 2023 film *Origin*, directed by Ava DuVernay.

Let me give you some historical examples of structural violence in action, as that will help to clarify exactly what it looks like. Many readers in the United States will have heard of the Jim Crow segregation laws that were enacted in the United States between 1877 and 1965. These laws reinforced a social hierarchy based on skin color and ancestry, which forced Black people onto the lowest rung of the ladder and kept them there through the use of violence and intimidation. This was "justified" by notions of white supremacy and the fear that Black people could "pollute" the purity of white people who occupied the higher rungs. Similar beliefs and fears also gave rise to the violence perpetrated against the Jewish community in Nazi Germany during the 1930s and 40s. As with the Jim Crow laws, this violence was enacted through government legislation, but in this case, it was crucially enabled by widespread antisemitism and an unswerving belief in the inherent supremacy of the idealized Aryan race.[19]

But structural violence doesn't just happen when laws and policies allow it. People can still be forced to occupy the lowest rungs of the social ladder even when there are laws in place that are intended to protect them. Today, structural violence rears its ugly head in racial slurs, in casual sexism and not-so casual misogyny, in a swastika spray painted on a Holocaust memorial, and in a pride flag set alight by a jeering crowd. When a Black man in the United States is pulled over by the cops because he's driving a classy car, that's structural violence. When an Algerian female athlete is relentlessly cyberbullied by powerful white celebrities who (wrongly) think she's transgender, that's structural violence.[20] When a presidential candidate makes fun of a disabled reporter and the audience laughs along with him, that's structural

---

19 The term "Aryan" has had various meanings throughout history, but by the early twentieth century, it had become associated with a superior (and totally mythical) race of people. The Nazis took up this idea in their claims that "true" German people were members of this "Aryan race." See "Aryan," United States Holocaust Memorial Museum, September 29, 2020, https://encyclopedia.ushmm.org/content/en/article/aryan-1.
20 Imane Khelif is the boss, fyi.

violence. And when that same candidate is caught on tape boasting about grabbing women's genitals and then proceeds to win the election (not once, but twice), that, my friends, is structural violence.

I'm sure you can think of other examples of structural violence and social hierarchies that exist in your own communities or in other parts of the world. And you may also be familiar with some examples in the biblical texts. One of the most blatant forms of structural violence portrayed in the Bible is the institution of enslavement. It's present in the texts of the Tanakh and the New Testament, almost from beginning to end. And while there are certain laws that forbid the "mistreatment" of some enslaved people (e.g., Leviticus 25:39–43), the practice of enslavement is rarely if ever explicitly recognized as a form of violence. For people living in ancient Southwest Asia[21] and the Roman Empire, it was part of the social structure—enslaved people were forced onto the lowest rung of the ladder, and that's where they were believed to belong. For some contemporary readers, this seeming acceptance of enslavement is both troubling and upsetting, yet it's surprising how often it's ignored or even excused in mainstream biblical scholarship. I'll delve more deeply into biblical enslavement in Chapter 5.

Other forms of structural violence in the Bible may not be as obvious as enslavement, but they're there, believe me. I've already spoken about the patriarchal foundations of gender-based violence, and patriarchy is certainly another source of structural violence, which relegates women (and some weaker men) to a lower rung on the social ladder. We can also detect structural violence in the language used to describe

---

21 "Ancient Southwest Asia" refers to the region that stretches between the Black Sea in the North, the Caspian Sea and Persian Gulf in the East, the Red Sea in the South, and the Mediterranean Sea in the West. It encompasses many of the ancient lands we read about in the Bible, including Mesopotamia, Canaan/Israel, Phoenicia, Philistia, and Egypt. I prefer "ancient Southwest Asia" to the more widely used "ancient Near East" because the term "Near East" was coined by nineteenth-century British colonizers who were interested in "exploring" the region. The less we have to do with colonizers, the better, imo.

the Indigenous communities of Canaan who are earmarked for annihilation during the Israelites' conquest of the land. I'll talk more about this last example in Chapter 3, especially the ways that language is used to frame these Indigenous communities as a polluting presence and a dangerous threat to the holiness of God's covenant people.

All in all, these four categories of violence offer a useful way to think about the violent deeds, words, institutions, and worldviews we'll be looking at in the rest of this book. As I said earlier, the categories sometimes overlap and merge with each other, but I think they're valuable to keep in mind, not least because they can help us recognize acts of biblical violence that are often overlooked.

In the following section, I'll explain the two main themes that will guide our journey through the Bible's texts of terror: power and emotion. I've chosen to focus on these because I believe they provide the most fruitful (and interesting) way for us to approach the topic of biblical violence.

## Power and Emotion

As you've heard me say already, power imbalances are the root cause of gender-based violence and structural violence: powerful people can take advantage of their power to act violently towards those who have less power than them. Power imbalances can also enable certain forms of physical violence to happen, including murder and human sacrifice, and the violent words of the powerful can sometimes pack a heavier punch than words spoken by the powerless. So when we look at violent texts, it's often useful to ask the following questions: who has the power in this situation? Where does their power come from? And how are they using (or perhaps misusing) their power to perpetrate violence? By tracing power dynamics in biblical texts of terror, we can better understand the root causes of violence and the wider meanings that it can carry.

"But what about emotion?" I hear you ask "What does that have to do with violence?" Well, one thing Agatha Christie and her crime writing siblings have taught me is that, along with power, human emotion often lies at the heart of violence, including its causes *and* its consequences. As I mentioned in the Infomercial, stories of violence are powerful and enduring because they show us how familiar, everyday human emotions such as anger, jealousy, fear, and shame can lead people to act violently. These stories also let us glimpse the equally familiar emotions that victims (and sometimes perpetrators) may feel both during and in the aftermath of violence, including fear, grief, betrayal, and remorse. The emotional foundations of violence can therefore allow us to better understand *why* violence happens and *how* it impacts those involved. And so, as part of our journey through the Bible's texts of terror, we're going to tap into the web of emotions that underlie the violence taking place.

Now, the emotions that drive people to violence are made pretty obvious in some biblical texts. For example, divine violence is often the result of God's "burning anger" and "fierce wrath" against certain individuals and communities, and human violence can erupt when the perpetrator is clearly angry or fearful. Readers can therefore easily see direct connections between the perpetrator's emotions and the violence they enact. But at other times, these connections aren't quite so apparent, and we're left wondering what emotions might have inspired the violence that occurs. In these cases, it's up to us as readers to dig a little deeper and search for clues that might reveal the emotional motivations underlying these violent acts.

A similar issue arises when we look for the emotional *consequences* of violence for both the perpetrators and their victims. Some biblical texts speak about these consequences with clarity and power, particularly with regard to victims of violence. We get access to the victims' perspective and can witness for ourselves how the violence has impacted them. Yet in other biblical texts of terror, victims' emotional responses remain hidden from view—we don't get to hear their voices or to "see" the outcome of the violence inflicted on them through *their* eyes. What's more, we're rarely shown the emotional effects of violence on the victims' families and communities or on the perpetrators themselves. And so, again, we need to put on our detective hats to search for clues that will show us the emotional aftermath of violence for *everyone* concerned. By doing so, we'll get a deeper insight into the significance of the violence and the meanings it may hold, both for the ancient writers and editors who wanted to share these stories and for audiences today.

Now, I know that, for some people reading this book, the emotional causes and consequences of violence will be all too familiar, either because they've experienced violence themselves or because they've witnessed it firsthand in their families and communities. They may also be aware through personal experience of the power imbalances that allow some forms of violence to flourish unchallenged. To these readers, let me first say that I'm truly sorry you've been impacted by violence. And I hope that you have access to the support you need and deserve. I acknowledge that some of the discussions in this book may be challenging to read because they hit a bit too close to home. And I also acknowledge that studying the Bible's stories of violence can be difficult for other reasons, too. The chapters that follow discuss texts that depict some truly disturbing forms of violence, and I'll sometimes need to dwell on these texts so that I can point out the violence that's both in plain view *and* hidden from sight. But I'll do my best to keep us all at a "safer distance" from this violence, and I'll never dwell on graphically violent imagery simply to shock you or to drive my point home. As I said in the Infomercial, we're on this journey together, and I'll guide you along the rocky roads of biblical violence until we arrive home safely.

## Road Map

Speaking of journeys, I'll end this chapter by sharing a map of where our travels will take us. I've been dropping hints madly throughout this chapter about our various ports of call, but it's probably helpful if I lay out the order in which we'll arrive at each one.

Before I begin, though, let me explain about the chapter format. In a nutshell, each chapter focuses on a specific type of violence, which is enacted through *one or more* of the categories of violence I described above (physical violence, gender-based violence, structural violence, and the violence of language). I'll give you an overview of where each type of violence can be found in the Tanakh and New Testament texts, and I'll discuss the various ways it can be portrayed, especially in light of our two key themes, power and emotion. In addition, I'll offer a deeper analysis of one or two biblical texts that depict this violence in a particularly enlightening way. I've called these analyses "case files,"[22] and it's here that we'll do some sleuthing to uncover how the texts shed light on the significance of violence, both in the biblical world and within readers' own lives and contexts today.

Our journey starts in Chapter 2 with stories of murder and killings, and the case file will investigate Cain's murder of his brother Abel (Genesis 4). Chapter 3 then focuses on the Bible's depictions of divine violence. There are a *lot* of texts to get through here, including those that portray the deity's involvement in murder, grievous bodily harm, warfare, threats and intimidation, and cosmic violence. The case file for this chapter focuses on God's complicity in genocide during the flood event (Genesis 6–9) and the Israelite conquest of Canaan (Joshua 6–11).

In Chapter 4, I turn my attention to a form of gender-based violence that's particularly prominent in the biblical texts: sexual violence. Again, there are a lot of texts to consider for this topic, but I've chosen Genesis 34 for our case file—the rape and abduction of Dinah, daughter of Leah and Jacob. Then in Chapter 5, I address the structural violence of enslavement, and I've chosen some of Paul's letters as the focus of our case file. Lastly, Chapter 6 takes a closer look at human sacrifice,

22 I'm channeling Nancy Drew here. Or maybe Miss Marple, given that I'm no spring chicken, I live in a village, and I do love to knit.

and our case file will be the sacrifice of Jephthah's unnamed daughter (Judges 11:29–40). The chapter also reflects on New Testament understandings of Jesus's crucifixion as a form of human sacrifice.

Two final things before we set off. First, the purpose of this book is to shine a light on the different types of violence depicted in biblical texts and to explore some of the legacies left by these texts in our contemporary world. It is not my intention to justify or excuse any form of biblical violence, and readers won't come away with a sense of relief or satisfaction that this violence is acceptable, reasonable, or just. With a few very rare exceptions, the violence presented in the Bible's texts of terror is awful and indefensible. My primary mission is to reassure you that it is okay to feel appalled by biblical violence, and it is okay to acknowledge that, in both ancient and contemporary contexts, this violence is not okay—it's never okay.

Second, I haven't been able to cover every type or instance of biblical violence—it would be impossible to do so in a single book. I therefore apologize in advance if I gloss over any biblical texts of terror that you think are vital to this discussion. I've chosen texts and topics that I believe have a lot to say about violence in the Bible *and* in the world around us. Hopefully, this book will equip you with the tools and the enthusiasm to research other texts of terror yourself.

Right, are you ready to go?

# CHAPTER TWO

# Murder

## "Thou Shalt Not Kill ... or Shalt Thou?"

"Thou shalt not kill" is one of the Ten Commandments that God gives to Moses (Exodus 20:13; Deuteronomy 5:17).[1] Its seemingly unambiguous prohibition of murder is also echoed in other texts in the Tanakh (e.g., Genesis 9:5–6; Exodus 21:12; Leviticus 24:17; Numbers 35:16–21). And in the New Testament Gospels, Jesus himself repeats this commandment (Matthew 5:21; 19:18; Mark 10:19; Luke 18:20) and identifies murder as an action caused by "evil intentions" (Matthew 15:19).

Despite these clear indictments, murderers and serial killers roam free in the biblical texts, and—like murderers today—they kill for a range of reasons, including anger, personal gain, religious zeal, vengeance, and self-preservation. Not all of these killers are caught or punished for their crime; indeed, there are times when their homicidal acts are given the divine seal of approval. So, to make better sense of this, we'll begin with our first case file—the murder of Abel by his

---

1 This translation is from the King James Version of the Bible. I'll usually rely on the New Revised Standard Version updated edition (NRSVue) when quoting biblical texts.

brother, Cain (Genesis 4)—and then we'll survey some texts that suggest the Bible's views on murder are a little more nuanced than "Thou shalt not kill" would have us believe.

## Case File: Cain and Abel (Genesis 4)

Genesis 4 recounts the murder of Eve and Adam's son Abel by his older brother, Cain. The story begins by introducing the brothers: Abel is a shepherd, and Cain is an agriculturalist who "worked the soil" (Genesis 4:2). One day, both brothers make an offering to God—Cain offers some "fruits of the earth," and Abel brings the "fat portions from some of the firstborn of his flock" (4:3–4). For reasons that are left unclear, "The LORD looked with favor on Abel and his offering, but on Cain and his offering the LORD did not look with favor" (4:4–5). In other words, Abel and his offering get a gold star from God, while Cain and his offering get a big fat F. Now, Cain is seriously hacked off about this, and he ends up killing his brother (4:8). But God discovers what he's done and tells him to pack his bags. Cain then departs to the "land of Nod" (literally "land of wandering"), which lies east of Eden, where he settles down, starts a family, and builds his own city (4:16–18).

Genesis 4 is essentially the Bible's first murder mystery. As such, it has a lot to teach us about murder and those who perpetrate it. So let's dive in.

### The Emotional Roots of Murder

Cain's murder of Abel is clearly driven by his emotions. After God shows favor to Abel and his offering, we're told that "Cain was very angry, and his face was downcast" (Genesis 4:5). Readers aren't told why God preferred Abel's offering; biblical scholars have come up with some interesting theories about this,[2] but I'm not sure it's all that relevant. What *is* relevant is Cain's response—he's angry and it shows; his "downcast" face says it all. The Hebrew verb used to describe Cain's emotions here (*chara*) literally means "to burn or be hot with anger"—in my mind's eye, I can just picture his fiery glower. Given what's just happened with the offering debacle, his rage may also be laced with feelings of jealousy and humiliation—he's been well and truly bested, and by his little brother, no less. Psychoanalyst Helen Block Lewis coined the term "humiliated fury" to describe this toxic blend of violence-inducing emotions, which occurs when people (often men) feel disempowered, disrespected, inadequate, and shamed.[3] This, I think, captures perfectly what lies at the heart of Cain's "downcast" face.

Now, technically speaking, Abel isn't the real cause of Cain's anger and humiliation: it was God who showed a preference for Abel's offering, and it was God's decision to make this preference apparent to the brothers. But Cain could hardly hope to win a fight with the deity, so like many real-life murderers, he chooses to unleash his humiliated fury on a victim who is weaker than him. In other words, Abel is an "easy target," and his murder gives Cain a (temporary) sense that he's regained his power and overcome his shame. This is another lesson we can glean from the story: murderers often prefer to "punch down" rather than "punch up" when they're venting their humiliated fury. They'll strike out at a victim who is below them on the social ladder because the people who've *actually* angered and humiliated them are too far above them to reach.

---

2 For example, some scholars believe that Cain's fruity offering was inferior to Abel's meaty offering (God preferred roast lamb to fruit salad). Other suggestions are that Cain did not perform the sacrificial ritual correctly or that he offered it grudgingly rather than gladly.

3 Helen Block Lewis, *Shame and Guilt in Neurosis* (New York: International Universities Press, 1971). I first read about humiliated fury in Jess Hill's powerful book, *See What You Made Me Do: Power, Control, and Domestic Abuse* (Carlton, VIC: Black Inc., 2019).

## Murder Is a Choice

Identifying Cain's humiliated fury might help us understand where his violence stems from, but it certainly doesn't excuse it. Indeed, Genesis 4 takes pains to emphasize that murder is never an inevitable consequence of powerful emotions. After noticing that Cain is brooding, God takes him aside and has a serious word in his ear: "Why are you angry? Why is your face downcast? If you do what is good, will you not be uplifted? But if you do not do what is right, sin is crouching at your door; it desires to have you, but you must rule over it" (4:6).

Here, God is essentially telling Cain that he can follow one of two paths. He can turn his back on his anger—it's not too late to walk away, and if he does so, he'll feel much better. The phrase in v. 7 that I translated "will you not be uplifted?" comprises one Hebrew word (*se'et*), which literally means "elevation" or "lifting up," and it also has a sense of "dignity" and "exaltation." In other words, Cain's "down-turned" face will lift—his frown will turn into a smile. Cain's other option is to hold on tight to his humiliated fury, but if he chooses *this* path, the consequences will be dire. Sin, it appears, is "lurking at the door," desperate for Cain's attention. This is such an evocative (and rather terrifying) image, which personifies sin as a predatory creature crouched in the shadows, waiting patiently to pounce.

God's warning to Cain is such a key moment in the story, because it says something profound about the storyteller's understanding of murder: it's a *choice* that the killer makes. Lethal violence may be inspired by strong emotions, like shame, jealousy, and anger, but it isn't inevitable, and it can be avoided by choosing to process these emotions in a non-violent way. I sometimes think about this moment in the text when I read news stories describing murders carried out "in the heat of the moment" or (even worse) as a "crime of passion," as though the killer's emotions rendered them less culpable and made their violence inevitable (or even excusable). The author of Genesis 4 would demur: killers who experience humiliated fury *choose* to act on the emotions that have caused *their* faces to be downcast. They choose the wrong path.

### Yes, You *Are* Your Brother's Keeper

The murder of Abel is recounted in the sparsest of details: "Cain said to his brother Abel, 'Let us go out to the field'. And when they were in the field, Cain rose up against his brother Abel and killed him" (Genesis 4:8).[4] Exactly *how* Cain killed him is left unsaid, but the murder happens so abruptly, giving readers the impression that it was sudden and brutal, like an ambush.

You'll notice that v. 8 twice refers to Abel as Cain's brother. I think this repetition serves to emphasize the relationship between the murderer and his victim, which in turn renders the violence even more terrible. Cain didn't kill a stranger—he killed his younger brother. The enormity of what he's done is stressed further in v. 9. God asks Cain, "Where is your brother Abel?" and Cain responds with the well-known line, "I don't know. Am I my brother's keeper?" The Hebrew word translated "keeper" (*shomer*) comes from a verb that means "to keep, guard, protect" and sometimes "to save life"—all the things that Cain failed to do for Abel.

Cain's "I don't know" is an out-and-out lie—of course he knows where his brother is. And "Am I my brother's keeper?" sounds like a smart-ass response, along the lines of "How the hell would I know? Sheesh, I can't keep tabs on him 24/7." Like oh so many murderers, Cain is lying to the authorities in an effort to evade justice. But deep down, I suspect he knows he's done something wrong. He orchestrated the murder in a place where there would be no witnesses. He appears to have hidden the body. And now he's telling fibs to cover up his crime.

---

4 The phrase "Let us go out to the field" is not included in the Hebrew text of the Tanakh, but it does appear in other ancient versions of Genesis 4:7 (e.g. in Greek, Latin, Samaritan, and Syriac versions), so it is often added to English translations, too. Without it, the start of the verse could be translated as "Cain talked to his brother Abel."

So when he asks God "Am I my brother's keeper?" I think he knows that the correct answer is "Yes, of course you are." But his humiliated fury led him to destroy his brother's life and to permanently sever the precious bonds of human connection. His guilt is writ large here, and his flippant response to God only drives that home even more.

## Listen to the Victim's Voice

God ignores Cain's words and tells him the game is up: "What have you done? Listen! Your brother's blood cries out to me from the ground" (Genesis 4:10). This verse is both eerie and poignant, and it again tells us something important about this storyteller's understanding of murder: we need to listen for the victim's voice, because even after their death, they can still bear witness. In other words, their wounds and the blood they've shed are signs (or evidence, if you like) of the violence perpetrated against them. Abel may have been murdered—his voice silenced by his brother—but his unjustly spilled blood can still be heard crying out from the ground. And Abel's blood is calling out to God, demanding justice on Abel's behalf. The Hebrew verb translated as "cries out" (*tsa'aq*) is used in other biblical texts to denote cries of distress and cries for help, particularly from those unjustly treated or oppressed (e.g., Exodus 5:15; Isaiah 19:20; Lamentations 2:18). God hears the cries of Abel's blood and, like any good detective, works out what has happened. I'm reminded here of those crime dramas and true crime documentaries where criminalists use various forensic techniques to find justice for victims (think *CSI*, *Silent Witness*, *Forensic Files*, etc.). In this respect, Genesis 4 is truly before its time, as it likewise reminds audiences that the bodies and blood of murder victims can "speak" on the victims' behalf by testifying to the violence inflicted on them and pointing a finger at the person who so brutally stole their life.

I'm glad this detail appears in Genesis 4, because it's the only place in the narrative that allows us a glimpse of Abel's point of view. We're told nothing about how he may have been feeling in the moments leading up to the murder. Was he aware of Cain's anger and resentment? Or did his brother's attack come entirely out of the blue? What emotions were going through his mind when his brother struck the first blow? We can only speculate here, but it's important to focus on the victim's perspective, not just the perpetrator's. Because if we don't, we run the risk of failing to recognize the full horror of Cain's actions. He betrayed his brother's trust. He caused him to feel terror and pain. He turned what should have been a place of safety for Abel into a place of death. And that has to be called out.

## Murder Always Has Consequences

In the following verses, God tells Cain, "Now you are under a curse and driven from the ground, which opened its mouth to receive your brother's blood from your hand. When you work the ground, it will no longer yield its crops for you. You will be a restless wanderer on the earth" (4:11–12). Abel's blood—his life force—has been "received" by the earth in a way that implies care and compassion; it's as though the earth is offering a safe resting place for Abel's remains. It might also suggest that the earth is seeking justice for Abel by severing ties with his murderer. Being a farmer, Cain has enjoyed a fruitful relationship with the land, but now this relationship is over. As God warns Cain, the land has turned against him.

Cain's dislocation from the land is so encompassing that it will no longer offer him a livelihood or a home: he is to become "a restless wanderer on the earth." While this might sound as though Cain is simply destined to lead a nomadic lifestyle, I think it means something far more profound. God is warning him that his fundamental connection to the earth—his sense of rootedness and belonging to home, family, land, and community[5]—has been irreparably shattered by his

---

5 Readers in or from New Zealand may be familiar with the Māori term *tūrangawaewae* ("a place to stand"), which I think perfectly captures what Cain is losing here. *Tūrangawaewae* are "places where we feel especially empowered and connected. They are our foundation, our place in the world, our home." See Te Ahukaramū Charles Royal, "*Papatūānuku*—The

act of violence. *He* doesn't belong because his *violence* doesn't belong. The lesson to be learned here is that murder can have deep emotional consequences for the perpetrator. Any relief they may feel after venting their humiliated fury is short-lived, indeed—their life and their relationships will never be the same. And while we later learn that Cain settles down, starts a family, and builds himself a city (4:17–18), I wonder whether he ever felt "at home" there or whether he was still afflicted by the restlessness and rootlessness that God warned him about.

Cain's response to God's proclamations definitely gives off some "poor me" vibes: "My punishment is more than I can bear. Today you are driving me from the land, and I will be hidden from your presence; I will be a restless wanderer on the earth, and whoever finds me will kill me" (4:13–14). In these two verses, Cain refers to himself seven times ("my, I, me, I, I, me, me"), but he doesn't mention Abel once. If he's feeling remorse or regret about killing his brother, it's difficult to see. And rather than dwelling on Abel's lost life, he frames the consequences of his crime in terms of what *he* is about to lose. His anxiety about being killed himself is, in my mind, a bit of a self-own, or "leakage" as a criminal behavioral analyst might say. In other words, Cain is inadvertently revealing something about himself that he'd prefer not to acknowledge: he's such a terrible guy that anyone who meets him would probably rather end his life than see him wandering the earth.

God's response to Cain's complaint sounds strangely empathetic: "Not so; anyone who kills Cain will suffer vengeance seven times over." Then, God puts a "mark" on Cain "so that no one who found him would kill him" (4:15). This statement raises two interesting questions. First, what is this "mark"? The Hebrew word (*ot*) simply means "sign," so it's clearly something visible (which makes sense if it's meant to deter people from harming Cain). Scholars have come up with a number of suggestions, including a scar or some tattoo-like marking on his

---

Land: *Tūrangawaewae*—A Place to Stand," Te Ara: The Encyclopedia of New Zealand, http://www.TeAra.govt.nz/en/papatuanuku-the-land/page-5 (accessed 19 November 2024).

skin, a horn (on his head), and even a dog who will accompany him and protect him. Or perhaps this sign is not intended to protect Cain at all; rather, it may serve as a "badge of shame" which warns those he meets about the consequences of murder ("Look what happens to people who kill").[6]

This mark also raises another question: why would God want to protect Cain's life? A number of other texts in the Tanakh demand the death penalty for killers (Genesis 9:5–6; Exodus 21:12; Leviticus 24:17; Numbers 35:16–21). But here, God is bending over backwards to ensure Cain's life is protected. I suspect that this may be God's attempt to prevent homicidal violence from spiraling further in the human community. But if that was the plan, it doesn't work. In the previous chapter, I briefly noted that Cain's descendent Lamech carries on his great-great-great-grandfather's tradition of committing murder. In Genesis 4:23–24, Lamech boasts to his wives, "I have killed a man for wounding me, a young man for injuring me. If Cain is avenged seven times, then Lamech seventy-seven times." Cain's initial act of murder seems to have triggered a chain reaction of ever-increasing violence and humiliated fury.

Lamech's violence reminds us that murder doesn't only impact the victim and the killer; it also has consequences for the wider community. This is as true today as it was back in the biblical period. Many readers will have witnessed communities being shaken by the aftershocks of grief, fear, and anger when homicide strikes in their midst. Sometimes these aftershocks can spark further violence and retaliation, as they did with Lamech. But at other times, they may jolt community members to peaceful action and activism in an effort to put *an end* to the violence and the injustices that have caused it. I'm thinking here of groups such as Black Lives Matter, Say Her Name, and Native Hope,

---

6 The "mark of Cain" also has a disturbing racist and antisemitic legacy, as it's been used to equate Black skin and Jewish heritage with Cain's shameful act of murder. See Eva Mroczek, "Mark of Cain," *Bible Odyssey*, https://ww.bibleodyssey.org/articles/mark-of-cain/ (accessed July 13, 2024).

which raise awareness of and demand justice on behalf of Black and Indigenous people who have been killed due to the structural violence of white supremacy and misogyny.[7] The actions of these groups remind me in many ways of the earth in Genesis 4, which gave Abel's blood a platform to cry for justice after his death.

### Case Closed ... for Now

Genesis 4 offers readers many fascinating insights into the Bible's understanding of murder, including its emotional roots, its relationship to power, and its lasting repercussions on the victim, the killer, and their community. We'll encounter these themes again when we look at other biblical stories of murder. But, as will become apparent, biblical murders are treated in a range of different ways, not all of which align with what I've highlighted during this case file. A lot of the time, murderers are judged according to their power and their emotional motivations for killing. So if you're ready, let's continue our murder investigation, and I'll show you what I mean.

## Murder and Power

In Genesis 4, it's clear that God doesn't approve of Cain's murder. But we'd be wrong in thinking God roundly condemns every murder that happens in the Bible. In other biblical texts, the deity is portrayed as giving certain people permission (or even orders) to kill, and when this happens, there's often a bit of a "nothing to see here" vibe in the narrator's depiction of the violence—unlike Cain, the killers face no serious consequences for their actions, and their murderous deeds may even be depicted as commendable and just. Nevertheless, when the

---

7 You can find out more about these groups on their respective websites. Black Lives Matter: https://blacklivesmatter.com/; Say Her Name: https://www.aapf.org/sayhername; Native Hope: https://www.nativehope.org/.

perpetrator's power to kill comes from a less godly source, then their violence is viewed in a far more negative light.

Let me offer you an example to explain what I mean. Many readers will have heard of Queen Jezebel, who makes several appearances throughout 1 and 2 Kings.[8] Jezebel is the Phoenician wife of Ahab, king of Israel, and in her role as queen, she enjoys a great deal of political power. She also has religious power, as we're told that she has close ties to hundreds of prophets who serve the ancient Southwest Asian deities Baal and Asherah (1 Kings 18:19). From the first time we meet her, it's clear that she uses this impressive power to cause Trouble with a capital T. She persuades her husband Ahab to turn away from God and worship Baal and Asherah (1 Kings 16:31–33).[9] She also tries to get rid of the religious competition by "killing off" the prophets who serve Israel's god (18:4). If that isn't bad enough, she uses her political power to frame an Israelite man called Naboth for a crime he didn't commit and have him put to death, all because he refused to sell his family vineyard to Ahab (21:1–16).

Now, Jezebel's many crimes don't go unpunished; after the deaths of her husband and her sons, the newly anointed king of Israel, Jehu, orders her attendants to throw her from a window. When she falls to the ground, she's trampled by his soldiers' horses, and her remains are then eaten by dogs (2 Kings 9:30–33). Her grizzly end fulfills the words of the prophet Elijah, who has already warned Ahab that "dogs will devour Jezebel by the wall of Jezreel" as a punishment for her crimes (1 Kings 21:23).

No one in the text mourns Jezebel's murder, and the reader isn't encouraged to either, because she is portrayed as a dangerous woman

---

8 Jezebel is mentioned in 1 Kings 16:31–33, 18:4, 19:1–2, 21:1–25, and 2 Kings 9:7–10, 22, 30–37.

9 The text appears to equate Jezebel's ethnic and religious "otherness" with her dangerous influence over her husband. This theme crops up in other biblical texts, where non-Israelite women are portrayed as having the treacherous capacity to lead Israelite men into idolatry and away from God (see, e.g., Numbers 25:1–2; 31:15–16; 1 Kings 11:1–8).

who misuses her power to commit violence. Even worse, the sources of her power are presented as questionable to say the least. Monarchic power belonged to Israel's king, but Jezebel has no qualms about using her status as King Ahab's wife to her advantage—if anything, she comes across as *more* powerful than Ahab. And her religious power is tied to her affiliations with the prophets of non-Israelite deities rather than with the "legitimate" prophets of Israel's god (1 Kings 18:19). The fact that she's a woman and a Phoenician woman to boot doesn't do her any favors in the patriarchal world of biblical Israel, where women's access to power was sorely limited. Readers may be forgiven for thinking that her biggest crime is having power in the first place *and* daring to use it. And because she does so, the murders she commits are roundly condemned.

But when we look at King Jehu and the prophet Elijah—two key players in Jezebel's story—we can see how the legitimacy of *their* power renders their own homicidal violence acceptable, or even commendable. To put it bluntly, they are both portrayed as the deity's hitmen. As a prophet commissioned by God, Elijah appears to have free reign to arrange the slaughter of 450 prophets of Baal (Jezebel's pals) in an effort to stamp out idolatrous worship in Israel. And Jehu, who has been chosen by God as Israel's new king, is more than happy to follow the deity's command to "strike down" the house of Ahab as vengeance for Jezebel's murder spree (2 Kings 9:6–8). All in all, Jehu murders hundreds of people, including all of Ahab's family and supporters (9:14–10:14) and an untold number of Israelites who are still worshiping Baal (10:18–25).

So Elijah and Jehu commit just as many murders as Jezebel. And like Jezebel, they target anyone who doesn't share their religious beliefs or who poses a threat to their power and authority. But there are some significant differences between them. As I've already mentioned, Jezebel's gender, her non-Israelite identity, and her loyalty to Baal and Asherah set her apart and render her (in the eyes of the biblical authors) a particularly dubious character, whose actions are judged by different standards than those applied to the God-fearing Israelite men, Jehu and Elijah. And perhaps even more crucially, Elijah's and Jehu's murders also have the divine seal of approval—the power to kill that is vested in them comes directly from God. As we'll see, this particular yardstick for evaluating murder is used in other biblical narratives where killings occur.

But the legitimacy of a killer's power is not the only thing that helps us distinguish between "good" and "bad" murderers. The Bible's evaluation of killers also hinges on *why* they use their power to kill—in other words, their emotional motivations for murder. In the next section, I'll go through a number of these motivations; what we'll notice is that some of them are treated a bit more forgivingly than others.

## Motives for Murder

### Religious Zeal

Religious zeal can be defined as an intense, unshakeable, and enthusiastic belief in the veracity of one's religious beliefs. Religiously zealous people are particularly intent on protecting, upholding, and championing their faith, often by undermining or demonizing other faith traditions. And all too often, religious zeal can be expressed through the use of physical violence, violent language, and the structural violence of intolerance and persecution.

As we saw in the previous section, Jezebel, Jehu, and Elijah all appear to be motivated by religious zeal, to some extent at least. But this terrible trio aren't the first murderous zealots we encounter in the Bible. When the Israelites start worshiping a gold statue of a calf during their wilderness wanderings (Exodus 32:1–8), Moses orders the men from the tribe of Levi to kill the idolaters in their midst: "Put your sword on your side, each of you! Go back and forth from gate to gate throughout the camp, and each of you kill your brother, your friend, and your neighbor" (32:27). Three thousand Israelites are subsequently killed, and Moses rewards the killers, telling them,

"Today you have been ordained for the service of the Lord, each one at the cost of a son or a brother, and so have brought a blessing on yourselves this day" (32:29).

A similar event also happens in Numbers 25, when the Israelites once again break ranks to worship other gods. On this occasion, the Israelite men have started to fraternize with local Moabite and Midianite women, and before you know it, they are all sacrificing and bowing down to a local deity, Baal of Peor (25:1–2). God, we are told, is furious, so when Phinehas the priest sees an Israelite man bring a Midianite woman into their camp, he takes a spear and kills them both by piercing them "through the belly" (25:8). God then rewards Phinehas with a "covenant of perpetual priesthood" because he was "zealous for his God" (25:13).

The Hebrew words for "zeal" and "zealous" come from the verb *qana*, which carries the sense of being angrily and passionately jealous. As I mentioned in our case file, anger and jealousy are a dangerous mix of emotions. And when they occur in the context of religious zeal, they can inspire the murder of those who choose their own path and their own god. What's more, the zealous killings carried out by figures such as Moses, Phinehas, Elijah, and Jehu appear to be rewarded by the deity. It's as though religious zeal for Israel's god is the biblical equivalent of a "get-out-of-jail-free card" where murder is concerned. And if that's the case, it leaves me feeling more than a little uneasy. History bears witness to the fact that religiously motivated violence does nothing to foster justice or flourishing within the human community; rather, it sows seeds of strife, stirs up intolerance, and ends the lives of far too many people of all faiths and none. We only need to think of 9/11, or the Rohingya genocide in Myanmar, or the swastikas decorating German churches during World War II to see the violent potential of religious zeal writ large.

There is another biblical murder that could be motivated by religious zeal, although some far more mundane reasons might also be at play. In Acts 7:54–60, Stephen, a deacon in the Jerusalem congregation of Jesus followers, is tried for blasphemy and stoned to death by an angry crowd. The men who plot his murder belong to various Jerusalem synagogues, and when they'd previously challenged Stephen's preaching, he'd outsmarted them with his "wisdom" and his spirit (6:10). So in a fit of pique, they falsely accuse him of blasphemy and bring him before the court of Jewish elders known as the Sanhedrin (6:11–15). Stephen defends himself against these charges in a very lengthy speech, but the crowd who are listening become enraged and drag him out of the city where they stone him to death (7:54–60).

Now, the people who carry out this stoning belong to Jerusalem's Jewish community, just as Stephen does, and they *might* be motivated by religious zeal if they genuinely believe a Jewish brother is blaspheming God.[10] But the men who originally laid these trumped-up charges appear to have been less zealous for the Lord than angry about Stephen besting them in a theological debate. If I were to make a guess, I'd say that these men were driven by a sense of humiliated fury, not unlike Cain. Their plot to get Stephen into trouble seems to be motivated by a desire to save face, lessen their shame, and reassert their power and status within their religious community.

### Self-Interest

Another common motive for biblical murders is plain old self-interest. Murderers in this category are driven to kill because, in their mind at least, they accrue some benefit from doing so. Very often, the perpetrator sees killing as a way to increase or hold onto their power. A particularly egregious example of this is recounted in the New Testament Gospel of Matthew, where King Herod the Great commands the murder of

---

10 At this point in time, followers of Jesus belonged to the Jewish community, and "Christianity" as it would come to be known didn't exist as a faith tradition separate from Judaism. In other words, Stephen's murder didn't spring from a conflict between Jews and Christians—it was a conflict between Jewish people who had different understandings of Jesus's significance to the faith. Jesus followers like Stephen believed Jesus was the long-awaited Jewish messiah, but Stephen's detractors did not.

all male infants in and around Bethlehem who are two years old or younger (Matthew 2:16–18). This horrendous event (often referred to as the "massacre of the innocents") takes place after a group of magi (astrologers) visit the king to ask about the recently-born child who they believe is the long-awaited messiah of the Jewish community. Fearing that this child will become a rival to his throne, Herod asks the magi to let him know when they locate this child so that he can "pay homage" (2:2). And although the text doesn't say as much, it's pretty clear that Herod's "homage" will involve doing harm to the child. Thankfully, though, he doesn't get the chance. After the magi track down Jesus to Bethlehem, they don't return to Herod, as they've been warned in a dream not to tell him Jesus's whereabouts (2:12). And Joseph, Jesus's father, is also told by an angel of the Lord to flee with his family to Egypt until the coast is clear (2:13–15). Herod, we are told, is "infuriated" when he learns that the magi have cold-shouldered him, and so "he sent and killed all the children in and around Bethlehem who were two years old or under" (2:16). The text doesn't mention that Herod is punished for these multiple murders; nor are we given any further details about his poor victims or their families.

Herod is not the first biblical king to murder his potential rivals and appear to get away with it. After the death of King David, his son Solomon takes various steps to consolidate his power as the new monarch. And one of these steps is ordering the murder of his elder brother Adonijah, whom he suspects is planning to make a play for the throne (1 Kings 2:13–25). Now, no one calls Solomon out for this murder, and he seems to get off scot-free, just like Herod. So could it be the case that powerful biblical men also have God's approval to commit self-interested murders?

You'll be relieved to hear that the answer to this question is no, they do not, at least not all the time. The most famous story of a king being punished for his self-centered, murderous deeds takes place in 2 Samuel 11–12. In chapter 11, King David rapes and impregnates a woman called Bathsheba, who is married to one of David's elite soldiers, Uriah the Hittite (11:3–4).[11] After learning that Bathsheba is pregnant, David attempts to avoid a charge of adultery by conspiring with his commander-in-chief Joab to ensure Uriah is killed during battle (11:14–25). He then takes Bathsheba as a wife and settles her into his royal palace (11:26–27).

But David's wrongdoings don't escape God's notice, who we're told is "displeased" by the king's behavior (2 Samuel 11:27). In 2 Samuel 12, Nathan the prophet tells David that God is going to punish him for both murdering Uriah *and* stealing his wife. Indeed, David's wife-stealing is mentioned three times by Nathan, while his murder of Uriah is only mentioned once (12:9–12). This might tell us something about Nathan's (and God's) priorities here. It's almost as though the greater wrong done to Uriah by David was the "theft" of his wife, rather than the taking of his life. Perhaps kings *can* sometimes get away with murder, but not when they're motivated by a desire to cover up adultery.

## Self-Defense

The motive of self-defense is rarely mentioned in the biblical narratives, but there are two occasions—both in the book of Judges—where I believe we can see it at play. What's particularly interesting is that, in each case, the killer is a woman, which might say something about this motive for murder being more common among those who lack social, religious, or political power. In Judges 4, the Israelites are at war with King Jabon of Canaan. One of Jabon's allies is a man called Heber, but despite this alliance, Heber's wife, Jael, ends up killing Sisera, Jabon's army general. Jael comes across Sisera fleeing the battlefield after the Israelite army gains the upper hand. She invites him into her tent for some refreshment and rest (4:18–20), but as soon as he falls asleep, she picks up a hammer and tent peg and drives the peg into his temple, killing him instantly (4:21). Israel goes on to win the battle, and the

---

11 I'll return to Bathsheba in Chapter 4.

prophet Deborah—Israel's current leader—sings a song of praise to God, where she refers to Jael as "most blessed of women" (5:24).

While this may not sound like a case of self-defense, you've got to hear me out. When Jael sees Sisera has fled the battle, she likely knows that an Israelite victory is imminent. This places her in a very vulnerable position—as the wife of an ally to the defeated enemy, she may know that she could easily become the target of Israelite violence, including sexual violence and/or enslavement. As I'll discuss in more detail in Chapter 4, various texts in the Tanakh confirm that Israelite troops regularly raped and enslaved enemy women during warfare. So Jael could be making a preemptive strike here (pardon the pun, again) to save her own life by joining ranks with the winning side.

The second case of self-defense occurs in Judges 9:50–56. To set the scene, the power-hungry Abimelech (who's from the Israelite tribe of Manasseh) is currently engaged in a series of military skirmishes (9:34–49). He's already killed many Israelites (both soldiers and civilians), and he's followed Cain's footsteps by murdering his own brothers (all seventy of them). When he reaches the city of Thebez, he sets out to burn down a tower in which the inhabitants are hiding (9:50–52). But out of the blue, a woman who is sheltering in the tower drops a millstone onto his head and crushes his skull, mortally wounding him (9:53). Abimelech calls out to his armor bearer to finish him off so that he can avoid the shame of being remembered as the man who was killed by a woman (9:54). Once he's dead, his troops go home, and the people of Thebez are saved (9:55).

We never hear another word about this unnamed woman—the shero of the day—but the text leaves us in no doubt that she's on the side of the angels, meting out divine justice to avenge Abimelech's own murderous violence. The narrator tells us, "Thus God repaid Abimelech for the crime he committed against his father in killing his seventy brothers" (9:56). But I think it's also important to consider the woman's personal motives, too. She and all the people of Thebez were trapped in a tower that was under siege, and a megalomaniac was about to set it alight and burn them all to death. She'd have been terrified and desperate, and I can only imagine how she might have felt when her eyes lighted upon that millstone and a plan started forming in her head. As a woman with no political or military power to confront Abimelech on the battlefield, her only option to protect herself *and* her townsfolk was to drop the millstone. I'm really glad she did.[12]

## Vengeance

Vengeance is another common motivation for murder, and there are many biblical figures who kill as a way to avenge a perceived wrongdoing. You'll recall that we saw this play out in Genesis 4:23–24, when Cain's descendent Lamech kills a man for "wounding" him and boasts that he will be avenged "seventy-seven" times.

In a number of biblical texts, homicidal vengeance is directed at those who have committed earlier murders. For example, both Gideon (Judges 8:18–21) and Joab (2 Samuel 3:27) avenge their brothers' murders by killing the perpetrators. Neither Gideon nor Joab appear to be punished; indeed, other texts suggest that killing the murderer of a family member was acceptable. Several biblical laws stipulate that the "avenger of blood" (usually the nearest male relative of the murder victim) is allowed (or even obliged) to kill the perpetrator (e.g., Numbers 35:19; Deuteronomy 19:11–12; cf. 2 Samuel 14:1–11). And a wider notion of blood vengeance is also laid out in Genesis 9:6, where God tells Noah that "whoever sheds the blood of a human, by a human shall that person's blood be shed." Things have changed a lot since Genesis 4, where the deity gave murderer Cain a "mark" to protect him from harm.

---

12 This is one of those very rare cases of defensible biblical violence (in my mind, at least), and I say that not because a woman is wielding the weapon but because of what's at stake here—the safety and wellbeing of an entire town. The narrative depicts Abimelech as a man who's on a murderous rampage, and he's already killed hundreds, if not thousands, of his fellow Israelites. Had the woman been able to stop him without the use of violence, so much the better, but that was unlikely to happen, given the circumstances.

Nevertheless, other biblical texts may leave us with the strong suspicion that murders driven by any form of vengeance are far from ideal; indeed, they may only make matters worse. We see this clearly in Judges 15, when Israelite leader Samson gets embroiled in an ever-increasing spiral of violence. After learning that his Philistine bride has been given by her father to another man, he gets even by setting fire to the Philistine people's crops (Judges 15:1–6).[13] The Philistines then retaliate themselves by murdering Samson's former bride and her father, and Samson responds with *further* vengeance by inflicting upon the Philistine people a "massive defeat" (vv. 7–8). It appears that the cycle of violence is destined to repeat itself when vengeance is a motive. And as is so often the case, far too many bystanders are caught in the crossfire.

Samson's acts of violence seem to be driven by his sense of humiliated fury: he feels dishonored and disrespected, first by his prospective father-in-law and then by the Philistines. These emotions also motivate vengeance-driven killings in other biblical texts. For example, King Saul orders the murders of 85 priests after he wrongly suspects that they have dishonored him through their misplaced loyalties to his rival, David (1 Samuel 22:6–19); he also attempts to kill his son Jonathan for the exact same reasons (1 Samuel 20:30–33). Elsewhere, the dishonor caused by sexual violence can likewise lead to murder, particularly when this dishonor is framed as something inflicted on the victim's male kin, rather than on the victim herself. In Genesis 34, Judges 19–21, and 2 Samuel 13, a woman's rape is the catalyst for subsequent homicides because her kinsmen feel that *they've* been dishonored and disrespected by her rapist's (or rapists') actions. I'll talk more about these three texts in Chapter 4, but for now, let me just say that masculine honor can be a fragile thing indeed, and when it's threatened or damaged, humiliated fury and violence often follow.

---

13 Samson's vandalism here is a serious act of violence in its own right—he is effectively destroying civilian Philistines' livelihoods and food supply. And the way he executes this vengeance (through a horrific act of animal cruelty—see v. 4) makes it all the more reprehensible.

# Aftermath

I've spent most of this chapter focusing on biblical murderers and their victims. But murder impacts the victims' families, too. This repercussion of homicide is mostly overlooked in the biblical texts—even Genesis 4 doesn't mention how Abel's parents, Eve and Adam, responded to his murder. But there are a couple of narratives that serve as heartfelt testimonies to the brutal desolation murder leaves in its wake. In 2 Samuel 18:33 (MT 19:1), King David has just heard that his rebellious son, Absalom, is dead—he was killed by Joab, David's commander-in-chief, following Absalom's attempts to usurp his father's rule. But rather than being relieved that his son's rivalry is at an end, David, we are told, "was deeply moved and went up to the chamber over the gate and wept, and as he went he said, 'O my son Absalom, my son, my son Absalom! Would I had died instead of you, O Absalom, my son, my son!'" This simple repeated cry is a powerful witness to the pain of a father who has outlived his son. And while David is more often remembered for his lengthy eulogy to Saul and Jonathan after their deaths on the battlefield (2 Samuel 1:17–27), I think this short verse speaks far more evocatively about the devastation of grief.

The other text I want to mention also involves David, but this time, it isn't *his* grief that's foregrounded. In 2 Samuel 21:1–6, he agrees to hand over seven of Saul's sons to the Gibeonite people as "payback" for Saul's violence against the Gibeonites while he was king. All seven brothers are brutally murdered by being impaled "on the mountain before the Lord" (21:8–9), and their bodies are left to hang there as a sign of their father's dishonor. Two of the victims (Armoni and Mephibosheth) are the sons of Rizpah, a former consort[14] of Saul.

---

14  Rizpah is referred to as Saul's *pilegesh* (2 Samuel 3:10). Biblical scholars aren't sure about the precise meaning of this Hebrew term (which is usually translated as "consort" or "concubine"), but it seems to refer to women who were "secondary wives" and who perhaps had fewer legal and social privileges than primary wives.

The narrator tells us that she goes to where her sons' bodies hang, lays out sackcloth on a rock, and remains by their side "from the beginning of harvest until rain fell on them from the heavens"—a period of around six months. During this entire time, she mourns their deaths and protects them from predators: "She did not allow the birds of the air to come on the bodies by day or the wild animals by night" (21:10).

The narrator gives Rizpah no voice in this narrative, but her actions are worth a thousand words. The care she shows to her sons in the aftermath of their brutal deaths speaks to her trauma and enduring grief. To my mind, she illustrates the dreadful and life-altering repercussions of murder for the families left behind. Her presence also stands as a powerful protest and counter-testimony to the cycle of violence that is so often initiated and perpetuated by those in power.

## So, Shalt Thou Kill or Not?

After reaching the end of this chapter, I'm sure you'll agree that murder in the Bible is a bit more complicated than "Thou shalt not kill" would have us believe. Some murders are approved by God and others not so much. And some motives for murder are deemed legit (e.g., religious zeal for Israel's god), while others may be frowned upon (e.g., self-interest or religious zeal for other gods). But however murder is framed in these biblical texts of terror, we'd do well to remember the lessons learned from Genesis 4: murder *always* has an impact on the perpetrators and their victims, as well as the communities in which it occurs.

In the next chapter, we'll take a look at even more murders, as well as other forms of violence, but this time, the perpetrator is none other than God. And as we'll see, the themes of power and emotion play just as big a role where divine violence is concerned

# CHAPTER THREE

# Divine Violence

Without exaggeration, I could probably fill a library with books about divine violence in the Bible; so trying to cover this topic in a single chapter has proven no mean feat. To keep things manageable, I've broken down the portrayals of God's violence into different categories—murder and grievous bodily harm, threats and intimidation, warfare, cosmic violence, and (our case file) genocidal violence. While I don't have room to mention every incidence of divine violence, you'll hopefully get a sense of the *types* of violence God inflicts and commands, as well as the deity's emotional motivations for this violence.

Before I begin, let me add three short caveats. First, my focus in this chapter is on portrayals of divine violence *in the biblical texts*. I'm interested to see how the writers of these ancient traditions understood and depicted their god as a violent deity. What I'm *not* doing in this chapter is reflecting on the nature of God *in the world*; nor am I making any claims about God beyond those written in the pages of the Bible. I'm not a theologian—I'm a biblical scholar by trade and a bit of an expert on literary depictions of violent perps, so that's what I'll stick to. And whenever I critique acts of violence that God is described as committing, my critique is leveled at the violence itself (rather than at God) and also, at times, at the biblical writers who include this violence in their depictions of the deity.

Second, and related to this, I am treating the biblical texts that depict divine violence (and all biblical texts, to be honest) as literary works, rather than traditions documenting historical events. I make no assumptions about whether the actions and happenings described in these texts actually occurred historically in the way they're presented. My main interest lies in unpacking how and why the ancient writers chose to portray divine violence in the stories they told. Whether we ought to treat these stories as "true crime," "crime fiction," or something in-between is a topic for another day.

Third, I appreciate that this chapter is decidedly one-sided, in that it only focuses on one aspect (the violent part) of God's multifaceted portrayal in the Tanakh and New Testament. The reason for this one-sidedness is that I'm writing a book about violence in the Bible, and I barely have enough words as it is to cram all the important stuff in. So let me just acknowledge at the outset that, while God is certainly depicted as doing violent things, God is also presented (often in the same biblical book) as a deity who strives for peace and justice and whose love, compassion, and mercy know no bounds. The editors and compilers of the biblical texts allowed all of these contrasting portrayals to sit side-by-side, perhaps in an effort to capture the emotional depth and complexity of their god. So while my discussion might feel disheartening in its relentless focus on divine violence, don't forget that what I'm describing is only one part of God's rich characterization in both the Tanakh and the New Testament.

## Murder and Grievous Bodily Harm

The biblical texts portray God inflicting various forms of violence (sometimes with fatal effect) on both individuals and communities. I'll start by summarizing some of God's individual attacks before moving on to the deity's use of violence against particular groups of people that occurs outside the context of war. As we'll see, the biblical God employs a creative array of methods and a range of co-conspirators to carry out these violent deeds.

## Don't Take It Personally, But …

On several occasions, God is depicted as directly assaulting individuals. Often (though not always), this is because the unfortunate victims have made some kind of mistake. For example, God sends fire to "consume" Aaron's two sons, Nadab and Abihu, after they present an offering that is contrary to God's command (Leviticus 10:1–3). And in 2 Samuel 6:6–7, the deity smites a man called Uzzah because he touches the ark of the covenant—a wooden chest that carried the tablets of the covenant and was also believed to hold something of the divine presence. The ark is being transported to Jerusalem on a cart pulled by oxen, and Uzzah reaches out to stop it falling when the cart lurches suddenly. But despite his good intentions, we're told that "the anger of the LORD was kindled against Uzzah" and he's struck dead on the spot, presumably because he wasn't entitled to touch such a sacred object.

On some occasions, God calls on various heavenly beings to help perpetrate the violence. In 1 Kings 22, for example, the deity sends a spirit to "entice" King Ahab of Israel (Jezebel's husband, if you recall) to wage war against the king of Aram. The spirit passes on a message to Ahab's prophets, telling them to let Ahab know that God will ensure his victory (22:20–23). Unbeknownst to his prophets, though, this spirit's intel is "fake news," and Ahab is duly killed on the battlefield, just as God intended (22:34–35). The deity also targets another king—Saul this time—by afflicting him with an "evil spirit" that causes him mental torment after he falls out of divine favor (16:14–23).

Other heavenly beings likewise help the deity inflict individuals with all manner of harm. In the New Testament book of Acts, for example, King Herod of Agrippa meets a sticky end during a public address to the people of Tyre and Sidon. As he speaks, some crowd members start calling out that he has "the voice of a god and not of a mortal!" Herod fails to set the record straight, so the angel of the Lord strikes him down "and he was eaten by worms and died" (Acts 12:20–23). And in the book of Job, the deity allows another member of the heavenly council—known as the Accuser—to do the dirty work.[1] God tells the Accuser about a man called Job who, in God's eyes, is "a blameless and upright man who fears God and turns away from evil" (Job 1:8). The Accuser isn't convinced and tells God that Job wouldn't be quite so "blameless and upright" if the deity were to pour some misfortunes down on his head. God accepts this wager and allows the Accuser to torment Job with a series of hardships and tragedies, including the loss of all his possessions, the killing of his children, and the infliction of a painful skin disease (1:13–19; 2:7–8). Despite all these adversities, Job, we are told, stayed true to his god. So basically, God won the wager, and Job's suffering was, by God's own admission, all "for no reason" (2:3).[2]

There's a final story that I should mention, which *seems* to portray divine violence against an individual, although the text is a little ambiguous. In Genesis 32:22–32 (MT 32:23–33), the patriarch Jacob is subjected to an all-night wrestling match with a mystery "man" who ends up injuring Jacob's hip during the scuffle. It's unclear why the wrestling takes place or what purpose it serves, and it's equally unclear who Jacob's opponent actually is. But many biblical interpreters suggest that Jacob is wrestling with either God or an angel—this is hinted at by Jacob himself when he names the place this event took place as Peniel (literally, "the face of God") because "I have seen God face to face, yet my life is preserved" (32:30 [MT 32:31]). But whoever this

---

1 The Hebrew word translated here as "Accuser" is *satan*, which later becomes used as a proper name for the figure of Satan. But in Job (and other texts of the Tanakh), the *satan* is not a figure of evil but a member of the divine council, under God's authority, whose role seems to be akin to that of a prosecutor or tester of faith. So we should think of "the Accuser" as more of a job title rather than a name. For an overview of the development of the figure of *satan*/Satan in the Tanakh and New Testament, see John Drummond, "Who is Satan?" *Biblical Archaeology Society*, June 11, 2024, https://www.biblicalarchaeology. org/daily/biblical-topics/bible-interpretation/who-is-satan/.

2 But Job doesn't suffer in silence, and I'll return to his response at the end of this chapter.

person is, his wrestling skills seem to be on par with Jacob's, and I'd declare this match a draw.

## You're All Gonna Get It

There are times when divine violence is directed against a group, a community, or even a nation. A well-known example of this occurring outside the context of warfare is recounted in Genesis 19, where God single-handedly destroys the sinful cities of Sodom and Gomorrah by raining down sulfur and fire from the heavens (Genesis 19:24–25).[3] And later, in the book of Exodus, God inflicts violence on the entire nation of Egypt. The country's leader, Pharaoh, is oppressing the Israelite people through enslavement and forced labor, and he has also introduced a policy of killing Israelite male newborns in an effort to deplete the community's population (Exodus 1:8–22). God sends the prophet Moses to Egypt in order to persuade Pharaoh that he should let the Israelite people leave. But Pharaoh doesn't listen to Moses at first, and that has a lot to do with the fact that God has "hardened" Pharaoh's heart (Exodus 7:3). In other words, God is making Pharaoh stubbornly immune to Moses's pleas. This seems a little counterintuitive—why would God send Moses to ask for the Israelites' release only to then make it harder for Moses to achieve this goal? The answer may lie in what God says to Moses prior to his first meeting with Pharaoh:

> I will harden Pharaoh's heart, and I will multiply my signs and wonders in the land of Egypt. When Pharaoh does not listen to you, I will lay my hand upon Egypt and bring my people the Israelites, company by company, out of the land of Egypt by great acts of judgment. The Egyptians shall know that I am the LORD

---

3 Lot's wife also appears to be a victim of God's personal violence during this event—she's turned into a pillar of salt after she looks back at the burning cities, despite being told not to (Genesis 19:26). I'll revisit Sodom and Gomorrah in Chapter 4.

when I stretch out my hand against Egypt and bring the Israelites out from among them. (Exodus 7:3–5)

In other words, Pharaoh's stubbornness will allow God to use various "signs and wonders" that showcase the impressive extent of the deity's power. The Egyptian leader's hardness of heart also gives God the perfect excuse to inflict punishments on Egypt that are a fitting response to the atrocities this land is currently committing against God's covenant community.[4]

The "signs and wonders" alluded to by God end up being a series of ten catastrophic plagues that impact *all* inhabitants of Egypt, not just the heart-hardened Pharaoh. These plagues result in all the Egyptian water sources (rivers, canals, ponds) turning to blood; infestations of frogs, gnats, and flies; a deadly pestilence that strikes all livestock; festering boils that afflict human and other-than-human animals; deadly thunder and hail that destroys everything it strikes; a swarm of locusts that ravages the Egyptians' crops; a deep darkness falling over the land for three days and nights; and lastly, the killing of all Egyptian firstborn humans and livestock (Exodus 7:14–12:30). Taken together, these plagues compromise the Egyptians' bare necessities—water, food, health, light—and also life itself. And regardless of the fact that the Egyptian populace (including women, men, and children) wouldn't *all* have been complicit in Pharaoh's oppression of the Israelites, they nevertheless pay the price for their leader's hardened heart.

After the final plague—the killing of the firstborn (Exodus 12:29–30)—Pharaoh's hardened heart seems to eventually melt, which isn't surprising given that his own son has died during this plague. So he tells Moses and Aaron that the Israelites are free to go, and Moses leads the people out of Egypt. But God isn't quite finished with Pharaoh and "hardens his heart" once again so that the Egyptian leader is inspired

---

4 Peter Enns, *Exodus for Normal People: A Guide to the Story—and History—of the Second Book of the Bible* (Perkiomenville, PA: The Bible for Normal People, 2021), 52.

to lead his army in pursuit of the Israelites. But it's simply a ploy: as the Egyptian charioteers chase the fleeing Israelites through the parted waters of the sea, God releases the waters, and Pharaoh's entire army is drowned (Exodus 14:26–31). Once again, God seems to be motivated by the desire to show *everyone* who the GOAT[5] really is: "I will gain glory for myself over Pharaoh and all his army, his chariots, and his chariot drivers. Then the Egyptians shall know that I am the LORD, when I have gained glory for myself over Pharaoh, his chariots, and his chariot drivers" (14:17–18).

While God appears to be fiercely protective of the Israelites, this doesn't mean that they are immune from the deity's communal acts of violence. Just as God is depicted as being angered by the people of Sodom, Gomorrah, and Egypt, so too does God get *really mad* at members of the covenant community when they start playing up. And play up they do. As soon as they leave Egypt, they start complaining—they're hungry, they're thirsty, the food's terrible, they miss Egypt, Moses is *so* annoying, etc., etc., etc. On more than one occasion, God becomes enraged at their shenanigans and threatens to "consume" them all (Exodus 32:10; Numbers 14:11–12; 16:45 [MT 17:10]). Thankfully, Moses always manages to talk the deity down, but the Israelites are nevertheless regularly afflicted with various divine punishments—including fire, plagues, and earthquakes—during their wilderness wanderings (e.g., Exodus 32:35; Numbers 11:31–34; 14:26–38; 16:48–49 [MT 17:13–14]; 21:6). Whenever they do something that betrays their lack of faith, God smites them as a reminder of who's really in charge.

God sometimes has help to mete out communal punishments. At times, these helpers are heavenly beings, such as the sword-wielding angel of destruction who inflicts Israel with a pestilence following David's disastrous census (2 Samuel 24). It's unclear why God is so mad at David for taking the census, particularly given the fact that it was none other than God who put the idea into David's head: "Again

---

5 Greatest Of All Time.

the anger of the LORD was kindled against Israel, and he incited David against them, saying, 'Go, count the people of Israel and Judah'" (24:1). This feels like a bit of a set-up, as though the deity is looking for an "excuse" to do some smiting.[6] The angel of the LORD is duly dispatched to execute David's punishment, and 70,000 Israelites fall victim to the pestilence.

This sword-wielding angel may fill us with fear and awe, but God's most intriguing assistants for executing divine violence turn out to be a couple of bears. Yes, bears. In 2 Kings 2:23–24, the prophet Elisha meets some little boys who shout at him, "Go away, baldhead! Go away, baldhead!" Elisha is clearly sensitive about his receding hairline, and he curses the boys "in the name of the LORD." Next thing you know, two she-bears appear and maul forty-two of the boys. God doesn't make an explicit appearance during this event, but Elisha's curse "in the name of the LORD" seems to imply that it's the deity who orchestrates the mauling. It's a horrifying story that doesn't appear to serve any real purpose (other than to stress that hair loss is a touchy subject for some men), but it does remind us that divine violence can occur without warning and in the strangest of ways.

Another intriguing agent of divine violence is the land itself. Although some of the prophets portray it as a victim of God's violence (e.g., Isaiah 24:1–6, 19–20; Habakkuk 3:6; Micah 1:4), several texts depict the land as a creature with a mouth and digestive tract, which gobbles up or spews out those who anger God. This imagery is used in Numbers 16, which recounts a particularly dramatic moment during the Israelites' wilderness wanderings. A few hundred Israelite men confront Moses and Aaron to complain that the dynamic duo are getting too uppity (it's a "who the hell do you two think you are?" kinda moment). Long story short, God singles out Korah, the ringleader

---

6 The author(s) of 1 Chronicles 21 (which recounts this same story) must have thought God's actions here were a little dodgy, too, so they say that it's the troublemaking Accuser (*satan*) who actually incites David rather than God (21:1).

of this rebellion, along with his followers, and "The earth opened its mouth and swallowed them up, as well as their households—everyone who belonged to Korah and all their goods. So they with all that belonged to them went down alive into Sheol [the realm of the dead]; the earth closed over them, and they perished from the midst of the assembly" (16:32–33). Just like that, they're gone—eaten up by the land, never to be seen again. This process is reversed in Leviticus 18:25 (which I'll come back to later), where the land is described as having "vomited out" its Canaanite inhabitants who are judged by God as being too sinful to remain living there.

## War

Warfare is a common form of divine violence depicted in the Tanakh—Israel's god is repeatedly portrayed as being involved in military matters, and one of the central metaphors used to describe the deity is that of a warrior and commander-in-chief of the Israelite and Judean armies. God is described as a "warrior" (Exodus 15:3) who is "mighty in battle" (Psalm 24:8) and who "marches in great might" while wearing robes stained crimson with the blood of the enemy (Isaiah 63:1–6). The deity is also repeatedly referred to as the "LORD of Hosts" or "God of Hosts," which literally means "LORD/God of [Israel's] armies" (e.g., 1 Samuel 17:45; Isaiah 9:19 [MT 9:18]; Amos 5:14–16; Psalm 24:10).

This warrior god metaphor isn't just a way to pay lip service to Israel's deity. Various texts in the Tanakh depict God being present in the fray of battle and actively engaging in combat on the Israelites' behalf. For example, during the wilderness wanderings, Moses reassures the Israelites that they need never be afraid of warfare because "it is the LORD your God who goes with you, to fight for you against your enemies, to give you victory" (Deuteronomy 20:4). Elsewhere in the Tanakh, God gives Israel's kings and leaders detailed instructions about military strategy (e.g., Joshua 6:1–5; Judges 7:9–11), engages directly in the fighting (e.g., Joshua 10:10–11; Judges 7:22; 1 Samuel 14:15; 2

Kings 19:35), and ultimately "delivers" the enemy into Israel's hands (e.g., Joshua 11:8; Judges 11:32; 1 Samuel 14:23). The battles of Israel are actually "the LORD's battles" (1 Samuel 18:17), and it is the LORD who guarantees victory on their behalf (2 Chronicles 20:15–17).[7] Human armies do play a role, but only insofar as they "come to the LORD's aid" on the battlefield (Judges 5:23).[8]

Now, there are plenty of occasions when the Israelites *don't* succeed on the battlefield—does this mean that Israel's LORD of Hosts can be "bested" by other nations' gods? Absolutely not. The writers of the Tanakh explain that Israel's failures on the battlefield are *their* fault, not God's, because their sins have driven the deity to withdraw support or even fight for the opposition. As Deuteronomy 28:25 explains, when the Israelites disobey God's commands, "The LORD will cause you to be defeated before your enemies" (cf. Leviticus 26:17). The prophets likewise use a similar logic to warn Israel that God will punish their idolatry and unfaithfulness by sending other nations to conquer them and carry them into exile.[9] In other words, God switches sides to teach the Israelites a lesson.[10]

---

7 The belief that a national god could secure military victory is not unique to the writers of the Tanakh; many ancient Southwest Asian lands also followed this line of thinking. This is illustrated, for example, in the Mesha Stele (also known as the Moabite Stone), which is an inscription dated to around 840 BCE. Written in the name of the Moabite king Mesha, it outlines the role of Moab's national deity, Chemosh, in securing Moab's military victory against the Israelites.

8 Aarnoud R. van der Deijl, *Protest or Propaganda: War in the Old Testament Book of Kings and in Contemporaneous Ancient Near Eastern Texts* (Leiden: Brill, 2008), 12.

9 For example, see Isaiah 9:8–12 [MT 9:7–11]; 10:5–6; Jeremiah 4:5–9; 5:15–17; Ezekiel 5–7; Hosea 10:13–15; 13:16 [MT 14:1]; Amos 2:4–16; 6:14.

10 This logic seems to crop up in some other ancient Southwest Asian texts, too, where a nation's defeat is at times explained in terms of the national god's displeasure at either the people or their king, rather than being taken as "evidence" that this god has been defeated by other (stronger) deities. For example, the Mesha Stele suggests that Israelite king Omri was able to oppress Moab for a time because Moab's god Chemosh was angry with his people

But God's wrath against the covenant community doesn't last forever. Once their punishment has been meted out, God switches sides *again* and ensures the conquest of their conquerors (e.g., Isaiah 10:24–27; 30:30–33; 45:1–7; Jeremiah 51:1). So just as the Israelites' losses on the battlefield remind them that God has the power to both defend them *and* defeat them, their enemies' downfall likewise drives home to everyone concerned that no emperor or deity can ever compete with the military might of Israel's LORD of Hosts. In other words, the biblical writers use Israel's successes *and* failures to showcase the deity's invincible power—God is always on the winning side, because God can never be beaten.

## Threats and Intimidation

Threatening words may seem a little small fry compared to some of the other violence we cover in this chapter. But as I mentioned in Chapter 1, language has the capacity to oppress, terrorize, and dehumanize an individual or group, and in the mouths of the powerful, words can be as deadly as any weapon. So biblical portrayals of an all-powerful God using threats and intimidation deserve our full attention.

Sometimes, God's verbal threats are aimed at empires, nations, and peoples who have been oppressing the covenant community. These threats are often relayed by the prophets, who describe with great relish the divine punishments that await Israel's enemies. In Isaiah 30:30–33, for example, God delivers a warning to the Assyrian empire, who, by the end of the eighth century BCE, had conquered the northern kingdom of Israel and sent many Israelites into captivity and exile. God's outstretched arm will strike Assyria "in furious anger and a flame of devouring fire" (30:30); the deity has even prepared an enormous

---

(lines 5–6). It's only when the Moabites are back in Chemosh's good books that the deity is said to have helped King Mesha gain victory in battle over the Israelites.

pyre on which to burn the Assyrian empire "with fire and wood in abundance; the breath of the LORD, like a stream of sulfur, kindles it" (30:33). And in the New Testament book of Revelation (more on which later), the prophet John of Patmos recounts numerous threats from God against the Roman Empire. One of the most striking of these is the threat of public stripping and burning leveled against a female figure called the Whore of Babylon, who's believed to be a personification of the Roman Empire. Babylon/Rome is accused of all manner of iniquities and abominations, and her punishment is described in sexually violent terms: "ten kings" (possibly Rome's allies) will come to "hate the whore; they will make her desolate and naked; they will devour her flesh and burn her up with fire" (Revelation 17:16). And a multitude in heaven will sing in celebration as they watch the smoke rise "forever and ever" from her stripped and ravaged body (19:1–3).

But God's threats aren't only reserved for other nations and empires—Israel is on the receiving end of a fair few itself. In both the prophetic books and the law codes, God intimidates the covenant community with warnings about the disastrous consequences of their sinfulness, including warfare, conquest, exile, sickness, starvation, and destruction of the land. God will execute judgments "in anger and fury" by inflicting upon them terror, panic, shame, and desperation, and they will become "a mockery and a taunt, a warning and a horror" to the surrounding nations (Ezekiel 5:15).[11]

If we try to pinpoint the emotions that underlie these threats against Israel, what becomes clear is that God is being portrayed as a deity who is utterly devastated and enraged by the covenant community's disloyalty and so uses threats and intimidation in an attempt to regain (or retain) their fidelity and love. In other words, the authors of these texts depict God as being prone to an all-consuming jealousy. This is also mentioned in Moses's warning to the Israelites about

---

11 To offer you a tiny taster of these threats, see Leviticus 26:14–39; Deuteronomy 28:15–68; Jeremiah 7:32–34; Ezekiel 5:5–7:27; Amos 8:9–14; Zechariah 14:1–2.

following other deities: "You shall worship no other god, because the LORD, whose name is Jealous, is a jealous God" (Exodus 34:14).[12] In other words, God demands complete and utter exclusivity from followers—or else. The fact that Moses refers to God using the moniker "Jealous" suggests that this may have been considered an integral part of the divine character. This speaks volumes about God's fierce devotion to the Israelites—it's as though the deity can't bear the thought of losing them so will go to *any* lengths to keep them. It also explains the threats and the violence God directs at other nations and empires who themselves threaten or endanger the community. But jealousy isn't an emotion we always think of in positive terms, as it's often associated with unhealthy or even hostile relationships. And I can't help but feel that God's "jealous" love for Israel sometimes comes across as a scary, controlling, *and* conditional love, which is as destructive as it is salvific.

The jealous nature of God's love for the covenant community is also writ large in texts that use the metaphor of adultery to accuse the Israelites of worshiping ("whoring after") other deities or forming alliances with other nations, rather than remaining faithful and "monogamous" to their covenant partner, God.[13] This metaphor is illustrated clearly by the prophet Jeremiah, who delivers the following threat from the deity to the people of Jerusalem, which warns them about their impending defeat by the Babylonian Empire: "I myself will lift up your skirts over your face, and your shame will be seen. I have seen your abominations, your adulteries and neighings, your shameless prostitutions on the hills of the countryside" (Jeremiah 13:26–27). The barrage of demeaning language and the humiliating threat of public stripping is intended to intimidate and shame the audience into understanding the enormity of their sin: infidelity to God.

---

12 God's jealousy is also mentioned in other texts, including Exodus 20:5, Deuteronomy 4:24, 5:9, 6:15, and 1 Corinthians 10:22.
13 The metaphor of "prostitution" or "whoring" to refer to the covenant community's infidelities is found in a number of texts in the Tanakh and New Testament. A few examples include Exodus 34:15–16; Leviticus 20:5–6; Judges 2:17; Psalm 106:39; Revelation 2:14, 21.

This metaphor of an "adulterous" covenant community is particularly prominent in Ezekiel 16 and 23 and Hosea 1–3, where God is portrayed as a cuckolded husband and Israel (or Jerusalem) is God's adulterous wife. Because of her infidelities, God threatens to inflict upon her a series of horrifying punishments, including entrapment, starvation, physical violence, disfigurement, stoning, and public stripping.[14] The husband/God also repeatedly degrades his errant wife by referring to her "lewdness," "defilement," "promiscuity," and "shame." And he reassures (or warns?) her that, after her punishment has been executed, there *will* be a reconciliation—she will be forgiven and the marriage will continue *so long as* she remains under his strict control (Ezekiel 16:62–63; Hosea 3:3).

A number of biblical scholars have pointed out the disturbing resonances this "marriage metaphor" has with the dynamics of intimate partner violence, where a husband's jealousy and humiliated fury at his wife's suspected infidelity leads to an outburst of violence, which is then followed by (an often temporary) reconciliation.[15] The relentless threats, intimidation, and denigration outlined in these chapters also remind me of the tactics used by some abusive partners to shame, subordinate, and control their victims. These tactics, often referred to collectively as coercive control, operate to reinforce the victim's powerlessness, keep them in a state of terror, and entrap them in the abusive relationship.[16]

---

14 There's nothing to suggest that these were standard punishments for women accused of adultery during the biblical period, but several texts do indicate that both men and women accused of adultery could face the death penalty, either by stoning (Deuteronomy 22:22–24; John 8:3–5) or, less commonly, by burning (Genesis 38:24).

15 One of the earliest (and best) explorations of this topic is by Renita J. Weems, *Battered Love: Marriage, Sex, and Violence in the Hebrew Prophets* (Minneapolis: Fortress, 1995).

16 For an accessible exploration of coercive control, I'd recommend Jess Hill's book, *See What You Made Me Do*.

Now, I acknowledge that this marriage metaphor is "only" a metaphor—it's a piece of imagery intended to explain to the Israelite audience why God is so angry with them. At the same time, though, I find it deeply concerning that the metaphor holds the abused wife accountable for her own victimization, as though she somehow "deserves" the violence she endures. This habit of blaming victims of intimate partner violence and coercive control is an all-too-common reality in many contemporary cultures. Victims may be accused (by family, friends, law enforcement, and the media) of "bringing it on themselves" when they try to disclose their abuse, as though they've somehow "driven" their abuser to perpetrate the violence. But the only people culpable for intimate partner violence and coercive control are the perpetrators, not the victims. No one—*no one*—deserves to be violated in this way, regardless of what they've done and not least of all by a partner who's supposed to love them and care for them.

And that leads me to the other thing that bothers me about this marriage metaphor. God's portrayal as a jealous, coercively controlling, and abusive husband could leave readers with the impression that intimate partner violence and coercive control *are* appropriate (or even divinely approved) responses to the alleged unfaithfulness of "real-life" partners and spouses, both in the biblical world and in contemporary culture. That is, the metaphor could be read as a prescription for the "correct" response to a partner's alleged infidelity, rather than as a highly stylized piece of literary rhetoric that's been shaped by the patriarchal (and misogynistic) culture within which it was created. This metaphor equates God's unchallengeable power and authority over the covenant community with the power and authority of a husband over his wife, including the power to control her and abuse her. That makes me very uneasy, not least because such a portrayal of God could have a deeply wounding impact on Bible readers (of all genders) who have themselves been victims (or who continue to be victims) of intimate partner violence and/or coercive control.

More than that, though, the prophetic marriage metaphor does God no favors by portraying the deity as an insecure and jealous husband who is consumed by so much humiliated fury that he threatens heinous acts of violence against the love of his life. You won't need me to tell you that intimidation and coercion are *never* part of a healthy, flourishing relationship. So the husband/God presented in this metaphor is, in my mind at least, a tragic figure whose relentless efforts to control his partner will not bring him happiness, peace, or authentic, mutual love. Meanwhile, the wife/God's covenant partner will only stay in the relationship through fear, intimidation, and entrapment rather than a genuine desire to see this partnership thrive. And that's a crying shame.

## Cosmic Violence

On some occasions, divine violence is depicted as being perpetrated on a cosmic scale. By "cosmic," I mean that this violence encompasses both the heavens and the earth. We've seen something similar before, when God sends an angel to strike down individuals and whole communities. But in a few biblical texts, heavenly involvement in the violence being done is far more widespread. And the best example of this is found in the New Testament book of Revelation.[17]

Revelation describes a vision received by the prophet John of Patmos, which he says was given to him by Christ. This vision shows John the events that are to unfold during the end times, when a final battle will be waged between God and the forces of evil. Now John doesn't receive a literal preview of what will happen; instead, the vision is filled with rich symbolism and otherworldly imagery, including monstrous beasts and dragons, cosmic battles between heavenly hosts of

---

17 I don't have space to do justice to the mind-boggling cosmic violence depicted in Revelation, but I'd strongly recommend you check out Robyn Whitaker's book, *Revelation for Normal People; A Guide to the Strangest and Most Dangerous Book in the Bible* (Harleysville, PA: The Bible for Normal People, 2023).

angels and the demonic armies of hell, lakes of burning sulfur, rivers of blood, and stars being swept from the sky by the tail of a giant dragon.

In the midst of all these extraordinary scenes is a portrait of the deity that mirrors so clearly the Tanakh's description of the LORD of Hosts. God is still protecting the community of the faithful by leading out an army against their enemies; only now, the army consists of angels and archangels, and the enemies are depicted as terrifying beasts and demons led by Satan himself. These supernatural foes are believed to represent the ongoing oppression of this community by the Roman Empire; but depicted as monstrous and demonic beings, the empire's power and the danger that it poses is magnified and made even more terrifying.

Nevertheless, the monsters, demons, and wicked individuals portrayed in Revelation are no match for God, whose emotions are fired up again to protect and deliver the covenant community. The deity's "wrath" is repeatedly mentioned, and it fuels the violence executed and orchestrated against those whose own violence and/or idolatry is viewed as a threat. In Revelation 16, for example, seven "bowls of the wrath of God" are poured out over the cosmos to inflict torment and death on innumerable idolaters and godless sinners. And in Revelation 14, two heavenly figures are depicted "harvesting" the earth with a sickle and cutting down the unrighteous, who are represented using the imagery of grapes on a vine. John reports that "the angel swung his sickle on the earth, gathered its grapes, and threw them into the great winepress of God's wrath. They were trampled in the winepress outside the city, and blood flowed out of the press, rising as high as the horses' bridles for a distance of 1,600 stadia" (around 180 miles or 300 km). This enemy-squishing "winepress of God's wrath" is mentioned again in Revelation 19, where a man appears, "dressed in a robe dipped in blood" and riding a white horse (19:11–13). Whoever this man is (and some interpreters think he may represent Christ), he's on the side of God and the angels. A sharp sword is coming out of his mouth "with which to strike down the nations," and he "treads the winepress of the fury of the wrath of God Almighty" (19:15). Then he cries out to the birds above, calling them to "gather together for the great supper of God, so that you may eat the flesh of kings, generals, and the mighty, of horses and their riders, and the flesh of all people, free and enslaved, great and small" (19:17–18). He then slays a multitude with the sword, and "all the birds were gorged with their flesh" (19:21) Oof.

The deity's violence depicted in Revelation is, again, metaphorical, and its intention is to reassure the beleaguered Jesus followers living in the Roman Empire that their warrior God has *not* been defeated and *will* conquer the enemy and the forces of evil. Better times are ahead, including the institution of "a new heaven and a new earth" and a "new Jerusalem," where the righteous will dwell with God, and "death will be no more" (21:1–4). Yet the blessings bestowed by God remain as conditional as they ever were, and the deity goes on to warn that faithless and "unclean" sinners will not be welcome in the new Jerusalem. Instead, "Their place will be in the lake that burns with fire and sulfur, which is the second death" (21:8; cf. 21:27; 22:15). Divine violence continues, even in this new world order.

## Case File: Genocidal Violence

Genocidal violence refers to violent acts that are used to intentionally destroy, in whole or part, a group of people who share a certain identity, be it their ethnicity, race, religion, geographical location, and/or political affiliation. These violent acts can include the deliberate killing of group members and the infliction of injury, emotional harm, and/ or other forms of violence that deny group members access to a livable life (such as destroying their homes, forcing them to flee, and cutting off their water supply or their access to food and healthcare). Genocidal violence may take the form of a one-off event, but it is usually carried out across a period of time and involves multiple and repeated acts of violence intended to deplete and destroy (both physically and emotionally) the victimized community.

In the biblical texts, God is portrayed as perpetrating or commanding genocidal violence, both in the context of war and in other situations, too. I'll start off by going over the flood event in Genesis 6–8 before turning to the conquest of Canaan, which we read about in the books of Deuteronomy and Joshua.

## The Flood

The flood described in Genesis 6–8 covers the entire earth and destroys all living things—it's an act of "uncreation," if you like, where God unravels the creative work carried out in the opening chapters of Genesis. In Genesis 6:5, we're told that "The LORD saw the wickedness of humans was great in the earth and that every inclination of the thoughts of their hearts was only evil continually."[18] God is deeply grieved and regretful about having created humanity (6:6) so decides to do something about it: "I will blot out from the earth the humans I have created—people together with animals and creeping things and birds of the air—for I am sorry that I have made them" (6:7). Only Noah and his family are to be spared, because Noah is "righteous in the sight of the LORD" (6:8). God directs him to build an ark and to gather into it pairs of every living creature[19] so that they will be preserved during the flood (6:13–21). After this is done, God sends a

---

18 Genesis 6:1–4 seem to suggest that God is already frustrated by humanity, even before their wickedness comes to light in v. 5. These first four verses tell a very strange tale about the "sons of God" (probably heavenly beings) having sex with the "daughters of humans." This results in these women giving birth to Nephilim, who are described as "the heroes that were of old, warriors of renown" (6:4). For reasons that are left unclear, God appears to be upset by this development and decides to limit the age-span of human beings to 120 years (6:3). Trust me, I'm as confused as you are, but it does seem to offer another possible reason for the deity's decision to uncreate creation. As an aside, in Numbers 13:32–33, the Nephilim are described as being giant-like in stature.

19 Or "seven pairs of clean and two pairs of unclean animals" if we go with Genesis 7:2–3.

cataclysmic deluge over the entire earth for forty days. The devastating impact of this flood event is recounted in three short verses:

> And all flesh died that moved on the earth, birds, domestic animals, wild animals, all swarming creatures that swarm on the earth, and all human beings; everything on dry land in whose nostrils was the breath of life died. God blotted out every living thing that was on the face of the ground, human beings and animals and creeping things and birds of the air; they were blotted out from the earth. (7:21–23)

These verses capture the totality of God's genocidal violence depicted in this story. Except for the people and animals sheltering in the ark, "all flesh" are drowned, both human and other-than-human animals alike. The horror of this extermination isn't dwelt upon in the narrative, and by grouping the victims together under the blanket term "all flesh," readers are kept at a distance from the violence because the term makes it harder to imagine the victims' individual faces and their personal experiences of the flood. On top of that, we've already been told that God sent the deluge because "all flesh" had "corrupted" the earth and filled it with violence—in other words, it's their own fault (6:11). Both of these factors encourage readers not to empathize with all those killed in the flood or to even recognize them as victims of genocidal violence.

The sheer scale of the extermination depicted in this narrative should take our breath away, not least because we're left wondering what it really achieved. After the waters subside, the deity has a moment of self-reflection and decides, "I will never again curse the ground because of humans, for the inclination of the human heart is evil from youth; nor will I ever again destroy every living creature as I have done" (8:21). This promise is reassuring, but it sounds as though God now realizes the flood hasn't ended the capacity for "all flesh" to corrupt and violate the earth. The human heart is inclined to evil—no amount of flood water can wash that away. So all God can do is promise to never "uncreate" the earth again. God even sets a reminder of this promise in the form of a "bow" that will hang in the sky when the rain clouds gather, just in case the temptation arises to blot everyone out again (9:14–16).

The story of the flood portrays a deity who is capable of genocidal violence, of that there is no doubt. To be sure, this violence isn't done lightly—God feels "regret" over the corruption of the earth, and the deity's heart is "grieved" at how creation has turned out (Genesis 6:6). God is presented here as one whose intense emotions can lead to extraordinary acts of violence. We've seen this theme crop up before, and it also recurs in the next part of this case file.

## The Conquest

Although God promises never to destroy "all flesh" again, it's obvious that *some* "flesh" does remain a target for genocidal violence. This comes out very clearly during the narratives about Israel's conquest and colonization of Canaan.[20] Earlier in the biblical narratives, God had promised Abraham that his offspring would inherit this land "for a perpetual holding" (Genesis 17:8; cf. 12:7; 15:18).[21] And after the exodus from Egypt, Moses assures the Israelites that God will fulfill this promise: the deity is planning to "defeat and subdue" the current inhabitants

---

20 Biblical scholars have various theories about whether the conquest of Canaan occurred as it is described in Joshua 6–11. Certainly, archaeological evidence doesn't support the idea that there was a wholescale conquest of the land over a relatively short space of time, as depicted in the Joshua narrative. As I mentioned at the start of the chapter, my main concern here isn't to determine whether the texts depict historical events in an accurate way; I'm more interested in how these stories of conquest speak to the biblical authors' understanding of a violent deity, as well as the political, ideological, and theological legacy that these texts have carried throughout history and up to the present day.

21 It's worth noting that the extent of the land being promised to Abraham varies in each of these three Genesis texts. Scholars have suggested that this may reflect the different traditions that were woven together during the creation of this narrative.

of Canaan "so that you may dispossess and destroy them quickly, as the LORD has promised you" (Deuteronomy 9:3–5; cf. 31:3–5).

What becomes apparent in the books of Deuteronomy and Joshua is that the Israelites' conquest of the "promised land" comes at a devastating cost to the Indigenous people already living there. This is spelled out plainly in Deuteronomy 7:1–2:

> When the LORD your God brings you into the land that you are about to enter and occupy and he clears away many nations before you—the Hittites, the Girgashites, the Amorites, the Canaanites, the Perizzites, the Hivites, and the Jebusites, seven nations more numerous and mightier than you—and when the LORD your God gives them over to you and you defeat them, then you must utterly destroy them. Make no covenant with them and show them no mercy.[22]

The phrase "utterly destroy them" is a translation of the Hebrew verb *haram*, which means "to destroy completely, dedicate for destruction, exterminate." The noun form of this term (*herem*) is used in a number of biblical texts to refer to the total slaughter of the enemy (both adults and children) and the dedication of these victims, along with all the spoils of war, to God.[23] In other words, the *herem* is an act of genocidal violence that's understood as a sacred act—an "offering" to the deity.

In the narratives depicting the conquest of Canaan, this act of *herem* is reported as taking place throughout the entire land. Joshua 6–11 offers a relentless depiction of genocidal violence, where God "gives over" or "hands over" each Canaanite city or community to Israel's leader Joshua, who then musters his troops and proceeds to

---

22 Moses gives a similar command in Deuteronomy 20:16–17, although this time, the Girgashites aren't mentioned.
23 Outside of the conquest narratives, the act of herem (sometimes referred to as "the ban") is mentioned in other texts, including Numbers 21:1–3, Deuteronomy 13:6–18 [MT 13:1–19], and 1 Samuel 15.

annihilate most if not all of the current inhabitants. At the end of Joshua 11 we read, "So Joshua took the whole land, according to all that the LORD had spoken to Moses, and Joshua gave it for an inheritance to Israel according to their tribal allotments. And the land had rest from war" (11:23). The following chapters in Joshua go on to detail how the newly colonized land is apportioned between the various Israelite tribes.[24]

The conquest narratives are not an enjoyable read. Genocidal violence is depicted vividly and unproblematically as being mandated and facilitated by God. And as we saw in the flood story, the victims of this violence—the Indigenous inhabitants of Canaan—are spoken of using blanket terms, such as "the nations" or "the people of the land," which again serves to keep them at an emotional distance from us. But even more disturbingly, the genocidal violence is presented as a "necessary" response to all these victims—in other words, they deserve it. To begin with, they're presented as a threat to Israel because they could tempt the Israelites to worship *their* gods, rather than the god of Israel (Deuteronomy 7:3–5; 20:17–18). And if that were to happen, the repercussions would be dire: "Then the anger of the LORD would be kindled against you, and he would destroy you quickly" (Deuteronomy 7:4). So in effect, the argument being made here is that the Canaanite peoples *must* be annihilated to protect God's relationship with the covenant community because Israelite eyes are prone to wander in the direction of other deities.

The idea that the Canaanites pose a "threat" to Israel is also portrayed through the repeated mentions of their "wickedness" and "abhorrent practices," such as idolatry, sorcery, soothsaying, and illicit

---

24 Later in the book of Joshua, we're told that some Canaanites manage to evade Joshua's acts of *herem* (13:1–7; 17:13). This explains why Judges 1:1–35 describes a number of Israelite tribes either engaging in various battles with the remaining inhabitants of Canaan or living alongside and/or enslaving them rather than "driving them out." But the fact that some Canaanites' lives were "spared" shouldn't deter us from recognizing the military activities described in these conquest narratives as depictions of genocidal violence.

sexual relations (e.g., Leviticus 18:24–29; 20:22–24; Deuteronomy 9:4–5; 18:9–14). The author of Deuteronomy explains that "it is because of such abhorrent practices that the LORD your God is driving them out before you" (18:12). The lawmakers of Leviticus go even further by presenting the Canaanites as a source of danger and a polluting presence: "Do not defile yourselves in any of these ways, for by all these practices the nations I am casting out before you have defiled themselves. Thus the land became defiled, and I punished it for its iniquity, and the land vomited out its inhabitants" (18:24–25). The Hebrew verb translated here as "defiled" (*timme*) is often used in ritual contexts to describe a person's loss of purity, either through contact with an unclean substance (such as blood or other bodily fluids) or due to sinful action (such as sexual immorality or idolatry). So by being identified as "defiled," the Indigenous inhabitants of Canaan are associated with sin, contagion, uncleanness, and danger. This is such a dehumanizing way to refer to *any* community, and it implies they are somehow deserving of the violence inflicted on them. And, as mentioned earlier in this chapter, the Canaanite people are described as being "vomited out" from this land, as though they were a repugnant, contaminating, or even poisonous presence; the violent conquest is thus reframed as a necessary step to "cleanse" or "purge" the land.

I'm sure you don't need me to tell you just how dangerous such rhetoric can be. It's been used often enough throughout history to justify all manner of violence (including genocidal violence) against different ethnic, racial, religious, and cultural communities. These communities seldom pose any threat whatsoever, but they are nevertheless painted by those in power as an odious *and* dangerous presence that cannot be tolerated or even allowed to live. This is the rhetoric that was used by European colonizers to justify the genocidal destruction of Indigenous peoples in the Americas, the African continent, and many other regions of the global South. It's the same rhetoric that underpinned the Nazis' systematic extermination of around seventeen million people whose religious or cultural identity, ethnicity, skin color, or disability marked them out as "subhuman," "vermin," or "life unworthy of life."[25] It's the same rhetoric that was drawn on during the 1994 Rwandan genocide carried out by Hutu extremists, who described their Tutsi rivals as *inyenzi* (cockroaches) in need of extermination.[26] And it's the same dehumanizing rhetoric that is currently being weaponized with devastating effect against Palestinian men, women, and children who live in the very lands in which these biblical narratives are set.

To hear this rhetoric being placed in God's mouth by the writers of these biblical texts makes me heartsore. And although some biblical scholars have tried to justify it by arguing that the Canaanite people must have been a wicked lot, I see no virtue in entertaining such an argument. There's no evidence to suggest that the people dwelling in Canaan who did not worship Israel's god lived significantly different lives to the Israelites themselves; nor is there any reason to believe that their cultural and religious practices were particularly "abhorrent" or "wicked." But even if they had been, that still doesn't justify their annihilation. Nevertheless, according to the writers of these biblical texts, such violence *was* justified because it served to protect Israel—God's "treasured possession" (Deuteronomy 7:6)—from the Canaanites' "dangerous" influence. Once again, the deity's relationship with the covenant community comes across as one that's based on fierce devotion, deep suspicion, and an unswerving capacity to use violence in order to ensure the community's loyalty.

---

25 The segments of society who were targeted by the Nazis' genocidal violence included Jewish, Slavic, and Romani communities, as well as people of color, disabled and mentally ill people, queer people, Jehovah's Witnesses, and political dissidents. The term "life unworthy of life" (German: *Lebensunwertes Leben*) became a key concept that operated to "justify" the mass killings that took place during the Holocaust.
26 "Rwanda Genocide Report," Human Rights Watch, last modified May 17, 2023. https://www.hrw.org/reports/1999/rwanda/Geno1-3-10.htm. Over 800,000 civilians (mostly Tutsi) were killed during this genocide.

### Case Closed … for Now

The flood and conquest narratives leave us with a question: why would biblical writers want to present their god as one who perpetrates or orchestrates genocidal violence? I can't say for sure, but perhaps these stories were used to remind audiences of the complexity and power of their deity. Genesis 6–9 portrays God as having total power and control over creation, and this power and control is used to both destroy "all flesh" *and* continue its survival through the family of human and other-than-human creatures so carefully preserved on the ark. The flood story also displays the range and intensity of the deity's emotions—grief, regret, and a determination not to give up entirely on humankind. And in the conquest narratives, God's emotions are at play, too, as we're reminded of that all-consuming "scary love" I mentioned earlier, which haunts so many depictions of God throughout the Bible. Such love can be creative and life-sustaining, but it can also be massively destructive towards the covenant community, the community's opponents, and even creation itself. So for better or for worse, these stories of divine genocidal violence—and divine violence more broadly—operate to reinforce the Bible's multifaceted portrayal of God, wherein love, anger, devotion, regret, compassion, jealousy, grief, and wrath sit side by side.

## Closing Thoughts

What are we to do with these biblical texts of terror that depict the deity's violence? How do we approach narratives of divinely orchestrated genocide, or metaphors portraying God as an abusive husband, or images of God "hardening hearts" and inflicting life-ending plagues that involve the killing of children? There are no simple answers to these questions, and a lot will depend on readers' own relationship with the texts. Some may find it easier to ignore these texts of terror and focus on portrayals of God that emphasize the deity's compassion and mercy. But allow me to suggest another approach that lets us engage with the divine violence depicted in the Bible, rather than skipping over it.

If we look to the biblical texts themselves, we find a long-standing tradition of protest and complaint against the violent acts of God. Abraham argues with God about the injustice of the deity's imminent destruction of Sodom and Gomorrah (Genesis 18:20–33), and Job protests vehemently about the deity's apparent infliction of multiple catastrophes upon him (e.g., Job 9:1–24; 16:7–17; 19:6–22). Neither man is prepared to let God off the hook, and neither is afraid to call out divine violence. This tradition of protest and complaint is also represented in the laments found in the book of Psalms, where the psalmists remonstrate about the injustice of divine violence and beseech the deity to bring it to an end (e.g., Psalms 6; 22; 44; 74; 79; 80; 88). We also find something similar throughout the book of Lamentations, where the lamenter (identified as Daughter Zion, the personification of Jerusalem) lists a litany of divine punishments that have befallen the city and insists that the deity's violence is excessive and unjust. These texts and others like them remind us that protests against God's violence are as biblical as the violence itself. So whenever we read any text of terror that depicts such violence, we need to remember that we're allowed to protest, too, not only against the divine violence presented in the texts but also against these same forms of violence that continue unabated today in so many communities the world over, including our own.

# CHAPTER FOUR

# Sexual Violence

Sexual violence refers to any act that impacts a person's sexuality through the use of coercion (e.g., physical force, intimidation, manipulation, or threats) and without their freely given consent. While it always involves the victim's sexuality, it is first and foremost an act of violence, rather than a sexual act. In other words, perpetrators of sexual violence are never motivated by sexual desire, love, or even lust; rather, they are driven by a desire to harm and demean their victim by exerting power and control over them.

Sexual violence in the Bible is a topic very close to my heart, not least because it's been the focus of my research since I began my postgraduate studies twenty years ago. At the start of that journey, I (rather naively) assumed that contemporary understandings of sexual violence would be very different from those we read in the Tanakh and New Testament. It didn't take me long to realize how utterly wrong I was. Today, sexual violence remains shrouded in many of the same harmful attitudes and misperceptions that we see in these ancient texts and their interpretations. Victims and survivors are still blamed, shamed, and silenced for their own victimization. Perpetrators are all too easily redeemed or exonerated. And the violence itself regularly goes unrecognized or is dismissed as "not that big of a deal."

With this in mind, let me lay out my roadmap for this chapter. I'll start with our case file—the rape of Dinah (Genesis 34)—which illustrates some recurring themes we find in biblical depictions of sexual violence, including victims' shaming and silencing, perpetrators' sense of entitlement, and the importance of masculine honor. Following the case file, I'll offer some examples of the different categories of sexual violence that we find in the Bible.[1] As you'll see, these categories overlap with each other to some extent, but they're a helpful way to understand the various dynamics that motivate and perpetuate this type of violence.

## Case File: The Rape of Dinah (Genesis 34)

Genesis 34 recounts the rape and abduction of Dinah, daughter of the patriarch Jacob and his first wife, Leah. At the end of Genesis 33, Jacob has just settled his family on some land next to the Canaanite city of Shechem (the home of the Hivite people). When Dinah goes out to meet some of the local Canaanite women, the prince of the city—who is also called Shechem—sees her and rapes her. He then decides he wants to marry her, but her brothers are having none of it, and they exact revenge for Shechem's actions in a spectacularly bloody way.

### Power, Privilege, and Redemption

Dinah's rape is recounted in Genesis 34:2: "When Shechem son of Hamor the Hivite, prince of the region, saw her, he seized her and lay with her by force."[2] The text suggests that the mere sight of Dinah inspires Shechem to commit the rape. This link between men "seeing" women and sexually assaulting them crops up in some other texts I'll

---

1 I'll save my discussion of sexual violence in the context of enslavement for Chapter 5.

2 Biblical Hebrew doesn't have an exact equivalent of the English word "rape," but here the violent and non-consensual nature of Shechem's actions is indicated by the verbs *laqak* ("to take hold of/seize") and *innah* ("to humiliate, abuse, violate"). The verb *innah* also occurs in other texts portraying sexual violence (e.g. Judges 19:24; 20:5; 2 Samuel 13:12, 14; Lamentations 5:11).

talk about shortly. More often than not, the men in question occupy positions of power—Shechem is a "prince of the land" (34:2)—and like many powerful men throughout history and up to the present day, they feel entitled to sexually access any woman they see, like, and want, even if it involves the use of force and regardless of the woman's wishes.

After he has raped Dinah, Shechem quickly decides that he loves her and wants to marry her, so he tells his father Hamor, "Get me this woman as a wife" (34:3–4). We shouldn't be fooled by Shechem's declarations of love here; while it's not unheard of for rapists to express affection (or even love) for their victims, the genuineness of these feelings is belied by their actions. As I said at the start of the chapter, rape has nothing to do with sexual desire or love: it's driven solely by the perpetrator's wish to exert power and control over their victim.

Shechem and Hamor head off to meet Dinah's family, and Shechem offers her father and brothers a generous bride price: "Let me find favor with you, and whatever you say to me I will give. Put the marriage present and gift as high as you like, and I will give whatever you ask me; only give me the young woman to be my wife" (34:11–12). The author might be trying to redeem Shechem's character here by casting him as a man who just wants to "do the right thing." Some biblical interpreters also follow this line of reasoning, and a few even suggest that we shouldn't think of Shechem as a rapist at all because he's such a decent chap, and he loves his girl.[3] But sorry, that's not good enough, because it's wrong to imagine that caring and generous men aren't capable of committing sexual violence. Men who rape come in all shapes and sizes—they can be family men, pillars of their community, and kind

---

3 For example, Gordon Wenham describes Shechem as "not your callous, anonymous rapist, so dreaded in modern society, but an affectionate young man." In *Genesis 16–50* (Dallas: Word Books, 1994), 317. And Jeffrey K. Salkin recognises that Shechem "violated" Dinah, but he also praises Shechem's great love for Dinah and refers to him as her "lover." In "Dinah, The Torah's Forgotten Woman," *Judaism* 35, no. 5 (1986): 284–289 (citations 286–87).

to their mother. So we shouldn't be fooled by Shechem's seemingly benevolent offer.

## Dinah's Defilement

Shechem isn't the only one to make Dinah's family an offer they can't refuse.[4] His father, Hamor, also suggests that Jacob's extended family should consider assimilating with the Hivite people in a more comprehensive way by settling in the city and intermarrying with the Hivite people (34:9–10). In response to this offer, Jacob says nothing (maybe he's giving it some serious thought). In fact, he hasn't said a word since he heard that "Shechem had defiled his daughter" (34:5). But Dinah's brothers are "indignant and very angry" at what has happened to their sister (34:7), and so they answer Shechem and Hamor "deceitfully" because Shechem had "defiled their sister" (34:13). Pretending to be open to this idea of assimilation, they nevertheless insist that all the Hivite men must be circumcised first (34:14–17) because it would be a "disgrace" for their sister to marry an uncircumcised man.[5] Hamor and Shechem gladly agree to this condition (34:18–24), but on the third day after the mass circumcision event, when the Hivite men are "still in pain," Dinah's brothers Simeon and Levi enter the city and kill all the males, including Hamor and Shechem (34:25–26). They retrieve Dinah from Shechem's house (where she appears to have been kept all this time), and then Jacob's other sons loot and pillage the city "because their sister had been defiled" (34:27–29).

You may have noticed that Dinah's father and brothers believe that she's been "defiled" (*timme*) by Shechem's rape (34:5, 13, 27). I

---

4 Spoiler alert: her family do, technically, refuse the offer, but in a really sneaky way.

5 In Genesis 17:10–14, God tells Abraham that all the males in his household should be circumcised as a sign of the covenant between God and Abraham's descendants. So what Dinah's brothers say here might be drawing on this covenantal promise, but the fact they use this sacred rite as a ruse to commit lethal violence is viewed by some biblical interpreters as shady to say the least.

mentioned in Chapter 3 that the Hebrew verb *timme* literally means "to defile, declare unclean." Here in Genesis 34, Dinah's defilement likely refers to the loss of her virginity outside of marriage. In biblical Israel, women were expected to remain virgins until they were married—their virginity was a sign of their social and spiritual worthiness, or "value," which enabled their father to secure a decent bride price from their future husband. So when an unmarried women lost her virginity, she was viewed as having been devalued, regardless of whether it was as the result of a rape.

The threefold mention of Dinah's defilement in Genesis 34 gives me pause for thought. It's certainly true that many victims and survivors do describe feeling "dirtied" or debased after their assault; rapists treat their victims with contempt, like an object that can be used and discarded, and this can, understandably, have a lasting impact on victims' sense of self-worth. But in addition to this, some victims and survivors also experience additional stigma because people (including their family members, friends, and wider community) may view them as having been "damaged" or devalued by the experience of sexual violence. In today's world, an "unchaste" woman (even one who has been raped) is *still* sometimes deemed less "valuable" and less "pure" (socially and spiritually). And that's just unforgivable, because these attitudes only serve to heighten victims' sense of shame and trauma.

## Rape and (Dis)honour

The response of Dinah's brothers to her rape and defilement is violent in the extreme, and biblical scholars are divided over whether their actions were justified. There's also some debate about the exact reasons for their intense anger. Some interpreters suggest that they're driven by anxiety over their sister's welfare, but I'm not really convinced. The brothers voice no concern for Dinah's wellbeing—in fact, after they rescue her from Shechem's house, the only time they mention her is when they complain to their father that Shechem has treated her "like a whore" (34:31). And they don't appear outraged by the moral wrongness of rape itself; after all, when they pillage the city of Shechem, they take all the women captive (34:29). It's likely that these women would have been raped and/or enslaved by Jacob's sons, as this was usually the fate of biblical women captured during conflict (I'll come back to this shortly).

My suspicion is that Dinah's brothers are angry because Shechem had sex with their sister without first asking her father's permission; by doing so, he disrespected and dishonored her father, and he also dishonored and shamed her brothers by showing them up as hopelessly incapable of protecting their sister and guarding her virginity. This, I think, lies at the heart of the brothers' humiliated fury when they hear about Dinah. Their sister has been treated "like a whore," and her defilement has caused *them* shame.

Jacob, meanwhile, is more worried about what the neighbors will think than he is about his daughter's welfare. He tells his sons, "You have brought trouble on me by making me odious to the inhabitants of the land, the Canaanites and the Perizzites; my numbers are few, and if they gather themselves against me and attack me, I shall be destroyed, both I and my household" (34:30). Jacob may have a point here: his sons' violence has likely put a target on his back. But even so, it's telling that, just like his sons, he expresses no concern for his daughter; and, like them, he seems more worried about how *his* honor and *his* reputation have been impacted by her rape. It feels as though this narrative is identifying the "real" victims of Dinah's sexual assault as her male family members. We'll see this theme crop up again in other biblical texts that depict sexual violence.

### Case Closed ... for Now

Throughout the Genesis 34 narrative, Dinah is given no words to speak, and we get no inkling about what she's thinking and feeling. What's more, other than her initial act of "going out" in v. 1, she has no agency; instead, things are done *to* her and decisions are made *for* her. We only really "see" her through the eyes of the men in the story:

she's the object of her rapist's "love"; she's the inspiration for a poten-
tially lucrative deal between the Hivites and the Jacobites; and she's the
daughter and sister whose "defilement" has caused her family great dishonor. In many ways, her treatment in this text reflects the experiences
of many rape survivors today who are likewise silenced by the shame,
blame, and stigma that's associated with sexual violence in their own
cultural contexts. And that breaks my heart.

All in all, Genesis 34 teaches us some valuable lessons about biblical understandings of rape, particularly as they relate to the themes of
power and privilege, honor and dishonor, and silence and shame. And
as you're about to see, these themes crop up time and again in other
biblical texts that depict sexual violence. So as soon as you feel ready,
let's move on and take a closer look.

## Power and Privilege

At its heart, sexual violence is all about power: perpetrators use their
power to hurt and control their victims, whose own *lack* of power leaves
them vulnerable to abuse. In some cases, this power imbalance is particularly pronounced. We saw this in Genesis 34, where Shechem—a
prince of the land—used his power and privilege to rape a woman and
demand her hand in marriage. But Shechem isn't the only powerful
man to behave in this way.

One of the most well-known examples of a powerful man using
his privilege to commit sexual violence is recounted in 2 Samuel 11.
The chapter opens with King David mooching around on the roof
of the palace. Suddenly, he "sees" a woman bathing and notices that
"she was very beautiful" (11:2), so he makes inquiries and learns that
she's Bathsheba, wife of one of David's elite soldiers, Uriah the Hittite.
Seemingly undeterred that she's a married woman (and therefore
strictly off-limits), he "sent messengers to get her, and she came to him,
and he lay with her" (11:4).

Biblical scholars and readers have long debated the precise nature of David's sexual encounter with Bathsheba—was it consensual or was it rape? For my part, I've no qualms about recognizing it as rape. Although David isn't described as being explicitly violent or coercive—he doesn't seize her or threaten her, as far as we know—the power imbalance between him and Bathsheba would have compromised Bathsheba's ability to say "no" without fear of the consequences. And sure, we're told that she "came to" the royal palace when David's servants summoned her (11:4), but that doesn't mean she went willingly—what choice did she really have? So given these factors, I think we can conclude that David raped Bathsheba.

Nevertheless, interpretations of 2 Samuel 11 don't always recognize David's treatment of Bathsheba as coercive or sexually violent, and if they accuse him of anything, it's adultery, not rape. Some interpreters even suggest that Bathsheba "tempts" the king by bathing in his line of vision. But this interpretation is deeply frustrating, because it effectively exonerates a powerful and privileged man of the crime he doubtlessly commits. The text doesn't say exactly *where* Bathsheba is bathing (inside her house or outdoors in a courtyard), but in a way it doesn't matter. When David sees her, he's free to make a choice: to keep looking or to look away and give her some privacy. The fact that he notices she is "very beautiful" suggests that he chooses to take a *long hard* look. Then, when he discovers she's married, he also has a choice: to leave her alone or to rape her. From start to finish, David's choices appear to be driven by his massive sense of entitlement to have anything he wants, even if it doesn't belong to him and no matter whom he hurts in the process. We might be reminded of Shechem here—another powerful man who "sees" a woman and decides that he must have her, whatever the cost.

Now, David is eventually punished by God for his actions in this narrative. But, as I alluded to in Chapter 2, when Nathan the prophet reads out the charge sheet, the king's primary sin is identified as adultery, not rape (2 Samuel 12:7–12). Just as Shechem "stole" Dinah's virginity from her father and brothers, David "stole" Bathsheba's sexuality from its rightful "owner" (her husband), and for that he must be punished. He further compounded his crime by having Uriah killed and then marrying Bathsheba himself. Bathsheba is never identified by the prophet as a victim of sexual violence. Nor is she given the chance to tell her side of the story. She only speaks once in the entirety of 2 Samuel 11–12, when she tells David "I am pregnant" (11:5). In Hebrew, that's just two words (*harah anoki*). Compare this to David, who (if my counting is correct) is given 112 Hebrew words to say throughout the two chapters (and none of these are spoken to Bathsheba). Having a voice appears to be the privilege of the powerful in this text of terror. Like Dinah, Bathsheba is surrounded and impacted by the words and actions of men, but her own experience of sexual violence is completely overlooked.

During Nathan's speech to David in 2 Samuel 12:7–12, the prophet delivers a warning from God about the punishments David can expect for his bad behavior. In v. 11, God tells David, "I will take your wives before your eyes and give them to your neighbor, and he shall lie with your wives in broad daylight." This particular punishment gets to the nub of David's sins: just as he "stole" another man's wife, so too will his own women be taken from him.

It's not too long before God makes good on this threat, and we learn that the "neighbor" in question is none other than David's son Absalom, who, as you may recall, tries to wrest the throne from his father. David has fled Jerusalem as he fears Absalom is about to attack the city, but he's left ten of his consorts to look after the palace (15:16). After Absalom arrives in Jerusalem, his advisor Ahithophel tells him to rape these women as a way to establish his authority over his father (16:20–21). Absalom follows this advice, and we read that "they pitched a tent for Absalom upon the roof, and Absalom had sex with his father's consorts in the sight of all Israel" (16:22). By raping these women, Absalom is furthering his claims to royal power—he's showing "all Israel" that *he* is in control of the royal harem and that his father isn't "man enough" to protect the women under his charge. Sexual violence therefore becomes a weapon used by men in their pursuit of political power.

When David comes back to Jerusalem and discovers what Absalom has done, he puts the women "in a house under guard" and does not have sex with them again. The women, we're told, "were shut up until the day of their death, living as if in widowhood" (2 Samuel 20:3). I get the feeling that David can't bear to see or hear the women, as they remind him too much of his own humiliation at the hands of his son. So he shuts them away—out of sight, out of mind. But this act of "shutting up" the women reminds me of the way that sexual violence is *still* so often hidden away and shrouded in shame, stigma, and silence. Like many victims and survivors today, the women are also "shut up" in the sense that they aren't given the chance to bear witness to their trauma.

The fact that these women's rapes were part of David's punishment from God is very discomfiting. David is the one who did wrong, but his consorts end up paying the price—and at God's behest, no less. The women are not only caught in the crossfire of a power struggle between two men (David and Absalom), but they also end up as collateral damage in the deity's quest for justice. We've seen this happen already in the case of Bathsheba, who likewise suffered as a consequence of David's sins through the death of her infant child. This is the structural violence of misogyny in action, where women's placement lower on the social ladder can leave them powerless and vulnerable to harm.

## Group Rape

Group rape (sometimes referred to as "gang rape" or "multiple perpetrator rape") occurs when the victim is sexually assaulted by two or more perpetrators. This form of sexual violence is a global phenomenon and occurs in a range of contexts spanning from military conflicts to social gatherings. The Tanakh has two narratives where group rape is threatened and/or enacted, and as you'll see, they bear an eerie resemblance to each other.

## Lot's Guests

In Genesis 19, two angelic messengers are spending the night in the house of Abraham's nephew Lot, who lives by the city of Sodom. The men of Sodom surround the house and demand that Lot brings out his guests "so that we may know them" (19:5). The Hebrew verb "to know" (*yada*) is a common euphemism for sex, both consensual and otherwise. But throughout this narrative, the men's violent words and actions make clear that they are planning to group rape Lot's two guests in order to dishonor and humiliate both them and their host, Lot.[6]

Lot attempts to appease the men by offering them his two virgin daughters: "Look, I have two daughters who have not known a man; let me bring them out to you, and you can do to them as you please; only do nothing to these men, for they have come under the shelter of my roof" (19:8). This is horrifying in and of itself, and it speaks to the point I made in the case file about biblical women's sexuality being the property of their male kin. Lot is technically within his rights to "give" these men his daughters' sexuality in an effort to protect his male guests. But his words here imply that male rape is viewed as a more heinous crime than the sexual violation of women. And as we saw with David's consorts, women's bodies are again used by men to further their own interests.

Thankfully, Lot's angelic guests swoop in to save the day; they drag Lot inside and blind the would-be rapists so they can't find the way to Lot's door (19:10–11). Lot, his daughters, and his guests escape unharmed (physically, at least). But as we'll discover later in this chapter, Lot's relationship with his daughters only goes from bad to worse.

---

6 This threatened rape of Lot's two guests has often been referred to by biblical interpreters as "homosexual rape," but I really baulk at that term, because it implies the men's actions were driven by same-gender desire. The text makes clear that the men of Sodom are motivated by their wish to hurt, humiliate, and dishonor both Lot and his guests. There's no sexual desire on display here (homosexual or otherwise), just a whole heap of male aggression.

### The Unnamed Consort (Judges 19–20)

Judges 19 is a variation on the theme presented in Genesis 19, in that it involves visitors to a house being threatened with group rape by a bunch of local men. In this version of the story, a Levite priest and his unnamed consort are lodging for the night with an elderly man in the town of Gibeah, which lies in the territory of the tribe of Benjamin. At some point during the evening, the house is surrounded by men from the city, who pound on the door and demand that the host "bring out the man who came into your house, so that we may know him" (19:22). Like Lot before him, the host is aghast and offers the men an alternative: "Here are my virgin daughter and his consort; let me bring them out now. Violate them and do whatever you want to them, but against this man do not do such a vile thing."

Now, as was the case with Lot, the host is within his rights (technically speaking) to offer his own daughter to the group of men outside. But he has no right whatsoever to offer them sexual access to another man's wife or consort. However, the Levite doesn't seem to care—in fact, he's apparently inspired by his host's suggestion, and he takes hold of his consort and pushes her outside. The narrator then tells us that the men of Gibeah "wantonly raped her and abused her all through the night until the morning. And as the dawn began to break, they let her go. As morning appeared, the woman came and fell down at the door of the man's house where her master was, until it was light" (19:25–26). Later that morning, when the Levite finds her, she's still lying at the door, "her hand on the threshold" (19:27). Perhaps she's pointing an accusing finger at the men inside the house who put her in harm's way then did nothing to help her.

The story of the unnamed woman is already horrific in the extreme, but it's about to get worse. The Levite takes her seemingly lifeless body home on the back of his donkey. Once there, "He took a knife, and grasping his consort he cut her into twelve pieces, limb by limb, and sent her throughout all the territory of Israel" as a means of summoning his countrymen (19:29). It's not clear at this point if she was still alive or if she had already died as the result of her night-long group rape. Either way, this further violation of her body is nothing short of a scandal: she's reduced from a living, breathing person to a mutilated symbol of the Levite's outrage. Her dismemberment is also a powerful expression of her total disintegration at the hands of men. And like the other female victims of rape we've met in this chapter, she's given no voice to protest or testify to the violence perpetrated against her.

When the Israelites gather to learn what has happened, the Levite stands before them and tells them, "The lords of Gibeah rose up against me and surrounded the house at night. They intended to kill me, and they raped my consort until she died" (20:5). His description of events is telling. He doesn't mention that he was himself threatened with rape, perhaps out of a sense of shame or trauma. That's understandable, and I'd never hold it against him. Nevertheless, his message strikes me as decidedly self-centered: the men of Gibeah rose up against *him*; they intended to kill *him*; and they raped and murdered *his* consort. All the wrongs have been done to *him*, not to the woman who was raped, murdered, and dismembered. And most telling of all, he omits to mention that *he* was the one who effectively handed her over to her rapists.

Nevertheless, the Levite's impassioned speech seems to work, and the gathered Israelites agree to wage war against the men of Gibeah. A bloody civil war ensues, and eventually, the entire tribe of Benjamin (to which the Gibeites belong) is also targeted. The cycle of violence spirals out of control, and countless Benjaminite men, women, and children are killed to the point where the tribe may not survive. To remedy this, the other tribes agree to abduct young unmarried women from the towns of Jabesh Gilead and Shiloh as wives for the surviving Benjaminite men (21:10–12, 19–24). So what began as the threatened group rape of one Levite priest ends with the group rape and murder of his consort and the abduction and marital rape of hundreds of women. Once again (and apologies for repeating myself), we're reminded that women are so often caught in the crossfire of battles fought between men.

## Rape During Conflict

The taking of the women from Shiloh and Jabesh Gilead is sometimes referred to by biblical scholars as an example of the ancient practice of "marriage by abduction." I'm not so keen on this term, as the use of "marriage" gives this event a veneer of respectability that it doesn't deserve. The women are forcibly abducted to become the wives of men from another tribe—they're unable to say "no" to this plan. So they are, in my mind, victims of rape as the direct result of conflict.

The rape and abduction of women during wars and civil conflicts is described in the texts of the Tanakh as a common practice in both Israel and the surrounding nations (e.g., Numbers 31; Deuteronomy 21:10–14; Judges 5:30; 21:10–12, 19–24; Lamentations 5:11); historical and literary writings also suggest it was a regular occurrence during the Persian and Greco-Roman periods.[7] As in Judges 21, this practice often resulted in the capture of women and girls as "war spoil" for the purposes of marriage and/or enslavement. One of the most egregious examples of this practice is described in Numbers 31, when the Israelites (who are still wandering in the wilderness) wage war against the Midianite people. The troops return victorious after looting the Midianites' property and abducting their women and children (31:9). Moses tells his men that they can "keep alive for yourselves" all the young girls who are still virgins (31:17–18). The phrase "for yourselves" strongly suggests that these "young girls" are to become "wives" of and/ or enslaved to their captors.

This is a shocking text (a text of terror indeed), not least because the girls' captivity and rape is commanded by Moses, a biblical hero

---

7 To offer just a couple of examples, Greek historian Herodotus (c. 484–c. 425 BCE) decries the savagery of wartime rape carried out by Persian armies, and Livy, a Roman historian (59 BCE–17 CE) likewise criticizes Roman troops for raping women, girls, and boys during their conquest of foreign peoples and nations. Interested readers can check out Elisabeth Vikman, "Ancient Origins: Sexual Violence in Warfare, Part I," *Anthropology & Medicine* 12, no. 1 (2005): 21–31.

and prophet of God. But the practice of taking female captives as wives is also presented as entirely acceptable in the laws that Moses later receives from the deity. Deuteronomy 21:10–12 tells Israelite soldiers that, if they "see among the captives a beautiful woman" whom they "desire and want to marry," they can rightfully take her home (cf. Deuteronomy 20:14). The woman in question has no choice in the matter—as a captive, she can do nothing to escape this fate. Again, this law should remind us of Shechem and David, who also "see" women and use violence in order to possess them sexually, regardless of the women's own wishes.

## Incestuous Rape

Two biblical texts describe acts of sexual violence that occur between close kin—siblings in one case (2 Samuel 13) and a father and his daughters in another (Genesis 19:30–38). Like other forms of sexual violence I've discussed in this chapter, incestuous rape always involves the perpetrator exploiting their victim's trust through the use of power and control.

### Tamar and Amnon (2 Samuel 13)

In 2 Samuel 13:1, we're introduced to three of David's children: Absalom, his sister Tamar, and their half-brother Amnon, who is David's oldest son. Amnon, we are told, "loves" the beautiful Tamar (13:1–2), which might remind us of Shechem's declarations of love for Dinah following her rape (Genesis 34:3). Given what goes on to happen, I suspect that Amnon's "love" for Tamar isn't as deep or as wholesome as he'd like us to believe.

Amnon orchestrates a private meeting with Tamar by pretending to be sick—he asks for her to come and cook him some health-restoring snacks, and she duly does as she's told. But as soon as they're alone, he says to her, "Come, lie with me, my sister." Tamar roundly rejects his advances and tries to talk him down, but Amnon ignores her, grabs hold of her, and rapes her (2 Samuel 13:14). His "love" for Tamar then curdles into a "very great loathing," and despite Tamar's pleas, he orders her to leave (13:15–17). She makes her way to her brother Absalom's house, "crying aloud as she went" (13:19). When Absalom sees her, he guesses what's happened, and he tells her, "Be quiet for now, my sister; he is your brother; do not take this to heart," and so she remains in her brother's house, "a desolate woman" (13:20). After two full years have passed, Absalom finally gets revenge on Amnon by orchestrating his murder (13:28–29), but we aren't told how Tamar feels about the death of her rapist.

Unlike the majority of biblical rape victims, Tamar is given a voice in this narrative to express her pain and trauma. And her trauma may be particularly acute given that her rapist is her half-brother—someone she presumably loved and trusted and whom she expected to feel safe around. The words she says to Amnon before her rape really capture her feelings of shock and betrayal:

> No, my brother, do not force me, for such a thing is not done in Israel; do not do anything so vile! As for me, where could I carry my shame? And as for you, you would be as one of the scoundrels in Israel. Now therefore, I beg you, speak to the king, for he will not withhold me from you. (13:12–13)

Tamar's reference to getting their father's permission to wed (13:13) may sound a little perplexing. Why would she want to marry the man who's threatening to rape her?[8] Perhaps she realized this might be the only way to avoid the shame and dishonor of losing her virginity *outside* of marriage. This is confirmed by what she says when Amnon tells her to leave after he's raped her: "No, my brother, for this wrong in

---

8 It's unclear whether sibling marriages were permitted during this period of Israel's history. While there are laws in Leviticus prohibiting incestuous relationships, including between siblings (Leviticus 18:6–18), we've no way of knowing when these laws became widely known and/or practiced in Israel.

sending me away is greater than the other that you did to me" (13:16). Her words drive home the power of those cultural beliefs that measure a woman's honor and worth according to her sexual chastity, and which also identify victims of rape as damaged and defiled. By raping her *and* rejecting her, Amnon effectively shuts down Tamar's protests and sentences her to a "desolate" life that's marked by the enduring stigma of sexual shame. The fact that her brother Absalom also tells her to "be quiet" (13:20) only reinforces her silencing by the men in her family.

### Lot and His Daughters (Genesis 19:30–38)

The rape of Lot by his two unnamed daughters occurs in the aftermath of the threatened group rape at Sodom (Genesis 19:1–11). After the two angels rescue Lot, they tell him to leave Sodom immediately as God is planning to rain sulfur and fire on the city. Long story short, a traumatized Lot flees to a remote area and lives in a cave with his two daughters. For some reason, the sisters believe that they're the only inhabitants left on the earth. So the elder daughter says to her sister, "Our father is old, and there is not a man on earth to have sex with us after the manner of all the world. Come, let us make our father drink wine, and we will lie with him, so that we may preserve offspring through our father" (19:31–32). The sisters enact their plan over two consecutive nights: they intoxicate their father and each one "lies with" him. Lot is unaware of what they've done (19:33, 35), although his suspicions may have been aroused when both daughters go on to bear a son, whom they call Moab (meaning "from the father") and Ben-ammi (meaning "son of my kinsman"). The clue, as they say, is in the name.

Now, I've noticed that Lot isn't always identified as a victim of incestuous rape in scholarly interpretations of this text; I've even seen his daughters' actions in the narrative described as "seductions" and as a "noble" way to continue the family line.[9] But we can't afford to ignore the

---

9 See John Goldingay, *Genesis* (Grand Rapids, MI: Baker Academic, 2020), ch. 16; Ronald Hendel, Chana Kronfeld, and Ilana Pardes, "Gender and

sexual violence that's happening in this text: Lot's daughters intoxicate their father to the point that he doesn't realize what's happening. They use alcohol to render him powerless and then abuse his trust in the most fundamental way. Like so many of the female victims in the texts I've discussed thus far, Lot is given no voice with which to express the trauma he goes through here. In fact, he simply disappears from the Genesis narrative after this event, as though he's been stigmatized and shamed by his rapes to the point of non-existence. So while I don't condone the way he treated his daughters earlier in the story, his treatment at *their* hands truly deserves readers' empathy.

## Closing Thoughts

In my experience, some people can find it confronting or upsetting to acknowledge that sexual violence exists in the biblical texts, particularly when they regard these texts as their sacred scripture. And scholars may also be reluctant to identify this form of biblical violence, or they may rationalize it away as an unfortunate but inevitable part of the ancient biblical world. But I think it's so important that we do acknowledge sexual violence when we encounter it in the Bible. Because if we don't, we allow this violence to exist "in plain sight" without challenging it or calling it out as an enduring form of injustice. And this in turn may make us less likely to recognize such violence when it happens in our own contexts and communities. Biblical texts of terror that depict sexual violence may be set in a world that's far removed in time and space from our own, but they have an enduring power to shape readers' attitudes and responses to sexual violence today. So as Bible readers, we have the opportunity to speak out on behalf of victims and survivors, both ancient and contemporary (ourselves included), and to call for an end to this all-too-common form of violence.

---

Sexuality," in *Reading Genesis: Ten Methods*, ed. Ronald Hendel (Cambridge: Cambridge University Press, 2010), 88–89.

# CHAPTER FIVE

# The Violence of Enslavement

Enslavement is a form of structural violence that we encounter repeatedly in the Tanakh and New Testament. Enslaved people were forced down to the lowest rungs of the social ladder because of their ethnicity, socioeconomic status, or political status (i.e., because they were non-citizens or prisoners taken captive during warfare). Kept in this social position through fear and brute force, they were disempowered, dehumanized, and left vulnerable to various forms of abuse and oppression. In the words of Greek philosopher Aristotle, the enslaved person was deemed little more than a "living tool" (Greek: *empsuchon organon*) who could be exploited for the benefit of their "owner," or enslaver.[1] Yet despite its inherent brutality, enslavement is rarely critiqued in the Bible, and its occurrence seems to be taken for granted by both the biblical authors and many later interpreters.

In this chapter, I'll go through some of the biblical texts that mention enslavement to illustrate how this form of violence is understood, represented, and often hidden "in plain sight." Along the way, we'll think about how our key theme of power is so pivotal to this form of violence being sustained and accepted. I begin with the Tanakh then

---

1 Aristotle, *Nicomachean Ethics* 8.11.

move on to the New Testament, where I present this chapter's case file, which focuses on some of the apostle Paul's writings about enslavement.

Before I begin, though, I want to address the oft-made claim that we shouldn't judge the Bible's seeming nonchalance toward enslavement by contemporary standards. According to this line of reasoning, biblical texts are a "product of their time"—the people who wrote them wouldn't have thought that enslavement was wrong or unjust because it was an accepted and entirely legal institution in both ancient Southwest Asia and the Roman Empire. In other words, biblical writers didn't know any better, so we can't blame them for being indifferent about enslavement or even giving it their seal of approval.

Now, for me, this argument simply doesn't wash. First, the fact that enslavement was part of everyday life in the biblical worlds doesn't mean it was any less violent or inhumane. Nor does it follow that we can't call it out as such just because it was considered acceptable and legal in these ancient contexts. We put ourselves on a very slippery slope when we entertain the idea that certain atrocities are beyond our criticism because they happened in the past and in a society where they were accepted and enshrined in law. I can think of many atrocities from more recent history—enslavement, colonialism, genocide, ethnic cleansing, apartheid, segregation—that meet these same criteria, and I'd hope these would *never* be dismissed in such an offhand way.

Second, to say that we "shouldn't judge enslavement" in the biblical worlds is essentially a coded way of saying that we shouldn't judge enslavers or the individuals, institutions, legal codes, and social ideologies that perpetuated, enabled, and validated enslavement during the biblical period. At no point in this process is any consideration given to the perspectives of those who were enslaved—their judgments and protests against this brutal and inhumane system are granted no audience, and their experiences of physical, emotional, and sexual violence are reframed and downplayed as the regrettable but inevitable outcome of ancient societal norms. Surely we can do better than that.

Lastly, to say that the biblical writers accepted enslavement because they "didn't know any better" lets them off the hook *and* does them a huge disservice, because it suggests that they lacked the moral compass to recognize the barbarity of enslavement despite witnessing it firsthand. Could they have done much to challenge or dismantle this nation-wide or empire-wide practice? Possibly not, but I wish they'd done *something*. As biblical scholar Stephen Patterson observes, the enduring power of enslavement "has always resided precisely in its assumed normalcy. No one ever thinks to question it."[2] As Bible readers, perhaps we can help to change this, not least because we live in a world where the shadow of enslavement remains ever-present.

All that being said, let's press ahead.

## Enslavement in the Tanakh

The practice of enslavement is mentioned repeatedly throughout the Tanakh. The patriarchs Abraham, Isaac, and Jacob were all enslavers (e.g. Genesis 12:16; 26:19; 30:43), while in the exodus narratives, the Israelites are themselves enslaved during their captivity in Egypt (Exodus 1:11–14; 5:6–18). And the legal codes preserved in the Tanakh lay down guidelines that appear to permit different forms of enslavement within the covenant community.

As in other ancient Southwest Asian lands, Israel regarded enslaved people as the legitimate "property" of their enslavers (Exodus 21:20–21). As "living tools," they often performed agricultural labor or domestic work, and enslaved women were also sometimes used sexually by their enslavers as a "wife" or consort (more on which later). The Hebrew term for an enslaved man is *ebed*, which comes from the verb *abad*, meaning "to serve, labor, work." Enslaved women are referred to as either *amahot* (singular *amah*) or *shefahot* (singular *shifhah*), both of which appear to be used interchangeably. Often, *ebed* is translated in

---

2 Stephen Patterson, *The Forgotten Creed: Christianity's Original Struggle against Bigotry, Slavery, and Sexism* (Oxford: Oxford University Press, 2018), 103.

English Bible versions as "servant," while *amah* and *shifhah* are translated as "maid" or "maidservant." But these translations don't quite hit the mark—unlike enslaved people, servants and maids are usually in paid service and are rarely considered the "living tool" or "property" of their employer.[3]

## Types of Enslavement

There are two types of enslavement mentioned in the Tanakh: chattel enslavement and debt bondage. In both cases, the victims were enslaved, but the reasons for their enslavement and their relationship to their enslaver were somewhat different.

Victims of chattel enslavement tended to be permanently enslaved unless their enslaver decided to grant them their freedom. As the "property" of their enslaver, they were treated like any other tangible possession—be it a house, land, or cattle—and could be passed on to the enslaver's children as part of their inheritance (Leviticus 25:46). The majority of victims were non-Israelite people who had been abducted from their homes or captured during warfare and either kept by their captor or sold/gifted to someone else. The law of Leviticus 25:44–46 stipulates that Israelites could acquire human chattel from the surrounding nations and from among the non-Israelite people who were currently living in Israel, but they were *not* allowed to subject their fellow-Israelites to the "harshness" of chattel enslavement (25:46). The law in Deuteronomy 24:7 doubles down on this prohibition and warns the Israelites that, "if someone is caught kidnapping another Israelite, enslaving or selling the Israelite, then that kidnaper shall die. So you shall purge the evil from your midst." In both of these verses, the brutality and injustice of chattel enslavement appears to be

---

3 If the terms "servant" and "maid/maidservant" are used in the NRSVue translation I'm quoting, I'll replace them with "enslaved man/person" and "enslaved woman," respectively.

recognized—it's "harsh," "evil," and worthy of the death penalty—but only when the victims are Israelites.

The enslavement of people from the surrounding nations also appears to be justified in Genesis 9:20–27, which is the first time the topic of enslavement is raised in the Tanakh. It's a strange tale, involving Noah, his son Ham, and an excess of wine. Ham sees his father Noah lying passed out naked (and drunk) in his tent, and when Noah finds out, he curses Ham's son, Canaan: "Cursed be Canaan; lowest of the enslaved shall he be to his brothers" (9:25). Noah then blesses his other two sons, Shem and Japhet: "Blessed by the LORD my God be Shem, and let Canaan be enslaved to him. May God make space for Japheth, and let him live in the tents of Shem, and let Canaan be enslaved to him" (9:26–27).

It's not at all clear from the text why Noah is so angry with Ham, but a fairly straightforward interpretation would be that Noah feels disrespected and dishonored (and maybe a wee bit ashamed and embarrassed) by the fact that his son has seen him naked. But what's less clear is why Noah chooses to curse his grandson Canaan rather than Ham. Some biblical scholars believe that this passage attempts to explain (or even justify) Israel's later practice of subjecting the Indigenous inhabitants of Canaan—who, according to the genealogy in Genesis 10:15–20, are descendants of Ham's son Canaan—to chattel enslavement.[4] In other words, the story reassures its audience that treating the Canaanites as human chattel is okay because Noah cursed their ancestor to a life of perpetual enslavement.[5]

---

4 David P. Wright, "'She Shall Not Go Free as Male Slaves Do': Developing Views About Slavery and Gender in the Laws of the Hebrew Bible," in *Beyond Slavery: Overcoming Its Religious and Sexual Legacies*, ed. Bernadette J. Brooten (New York: Palgrave Macmillan, 2010), 139; Matthias Winkler, "The Ancestors' Masculinities in Genesis," *Journal for the Study of the Old Testament* 46, no. 2 (2021): 273–74.

5 "Noah's curse" of Canaan has a long and shameful history of being misused by European and North American pro-slavery campaigners to justify the enslavement of Black people. See Kevin Burrell, "Slavery, the Hebrew Bible

The other form of enslavement described in the Tanakh—debt bondage—*did* allow Israelites to enslave each other, but only in certain circumstances. Debt bondage occurred when a person couldn't pay off a debt, and so they worked for their creditor (either a fellow Israelite or a non-Israelite living in Israel) as a means of paying them back. In other words, the debtor "sold" themselves to their creditor until the debt was paid off or their creditor released them (see Leviticus 25:39–43, 47–54). This form of enslavement was no less brutal than chattel enslavement: the person's rights were limited, they were not free to leave, and there was no guarantee that their creditor/enslaver would treat them fairly or decently. Israelites in financial straits were also sometimes compelled to sell their children into enslavement in order to pay off their debt (e.g., Exodus 21:7; 2 Kings 4:1; Nehemiah 5:5).

### Sexual Subjugation and Enslavement

Enslaved women and girls were particularly vulnerable to sexual exploitation at the hands of their enslavers. As I mentioned in Chapter 4, women and girls in the biblical world were regarded as male sexual property, but this is made even more apparent in the context of enslavement. For example, Exodus 21:7–11 lays out the rules around the treatment of a woman (or girl) whose father has sold her to an enslaver as a wife or consort. If she "does not please" her enslaver, he is not allowed to sell her as human chattel; instead, he can either keep her, give her to his son as a wife, or free her after her family have "redeemed" her (i.e., paid for her to be freed). In essence, the woman (or girl) has *no* control over who has sexual access to her body.

This practice of taking an enslaved woman as a wife is also mentioned in Genesis 16, where Sarai instructs her husband Abram to have sex with Hagar, an enslaved Egyptian woman (or girl), in order to get

and the Development of Racial Theories in the Nineteenth Century," *Religions* 12, no. 9: 742. https://doi.org/10.3390/rel12090742 (open access).

her pregnant.[6] Sarai appears unable to have children herself, so she "gives" Hagar to Abram as a wife, and he proceeds to impregnate her (16:1–4). Hagar eventually gives birth to a son called Ishmael, who would be regarded as the legitimate son of both Sarai and Abram— Hagar has no maternal rights in this arrangement.

The violence implicit in Hagar's treatment is often overlooked by biblical interpreters, who focus more on the long-awaited promise of a son for Abram. But we can't afford to ignore the fact that, as a non-Israelite enslaved woman, Hagar is given no say in what happens to her own body. Abram and Sarai intend to use her—or more precisely, use her womb—to bear a child, whether she wants them to or not. *Their* power as her enslavers renders *her* completely powerless—she's simply a piece of property (a "living tool") to be used to her enslavers' advantage.

Some readers might find it particularly disturbing that Sarai is complicit in another woman's sexual subjugation. But we need to remember that Sarai is childless, and she lives in a patriarchal world where a woman's social worth and status were dependent to a large extent on her capacity to bear sons who'd continue the family line.[7] Motherhood, then, was a means by which women could access even a little bit of power. Women like Sarai who were unable to bear children

---

6 Abram (whose name means "exalted ancestor") has his name changed by God to Abraham ("ancestor of a multitude") in Genesis 17:5 when God makes a covenant with him and promises that he will be "the ancestor of a multitude of nations" (17:4). God also renames Sarai ("princess") as Sarah ("princess, noblewoman") in 17:15.

7 We should also remember that Sarai has already learned from her husband that women's bodies can be used to further the interests of those more powerful than them. Earlier in their marriage, Abram allows Sarai to be taken into the Egyptian pharaoh's harem in an effort to protect his own safety (Genesis 12:10–20). Abram benefits greatly from this scheme—because of Sarai, the pharaoh "dealt well with Abram, and he had sheep, oxen, male donkeys, enslaved men and women, female donkeys, and camels" (12:16). What Sarai thought about this episode is not reported, nor do we hear her point of view when Abraham pulls a similar stunt later in Genesis 20.

(especially sons) would have been viewed as less worthy and less valuable to her family and community. By using Hagar to "obtain" a son for herself and Abraham (Genesis 16:2), Sarai is therefore bolstering her own power and social status. As womanist biblical scholar Wilda Gafney observes, Sarai "is free; she has some societal privilege as Abraham's woman and Hagar's mistress. But she is still an infertile woman in a male-dominated world, both of which imperil her status; she seeks to attain/restore her status on and in Hagar's body."[8] This *in no way* excuses Sarai's mistreatment of Hagar, but it might help us get a better sense of *why* she does so.

Sarai's treatment of Hagar is replicated a few generations later by Jacob's wives Rachel and Leah. Similar to Sarai, Rachel and Leah are feeling under pressure to produce sons for their husband, so they give him "their" enslaved women, Bilhah and Zilpah, as wives (Genesis 30:1–13). Bilhah and Zilpah (like Hagar before them) have no choice but to comply with these childbearing arrangements—as enslaved women, their bodies are not their own. Their status as wives doesn't replace or negate their status as human chattel—they do not gain their freedom after they're married to Jacob.

Enslaved men in ancient Southwest Asia may also have been subjected to sexual violence. Genesis 39:6–20 recounts Joseph's experience of sexual harassment and attempted rape while he's enslaved in Egypt, and it's likely that this also happened to other enslaved men throughout the ancient world. Joseph is sold by his big brothers to some passing traders (37:25–28),[9] who take him to Egypt and sell him on to a man called Potiphar, one of Pharaoh's officials (Genesis 37:36). Potiphar's wife repeatedly harasses Joseph to have sex with her (39:7–10), and when he rejects her once too often, she accuses of him

---

8 See Wilda C. Gafney, *Womanist Midrash: A Reintroduction to the Women of the Torah and the Throne* (Westminster John Knox, 2017), 41.

9 A little confusingly, Genesis 37:25 identifies the traders as Ishmaelites, whereas v. 28 refers to them as Midianites. This might simply be the result of two separate traditions of this story having been woven together a bit awkwardly here.

of trying to rape *her* (39:11–18). Her accusations are believed (no doubt owing to her superior status), and Joseph is then imprisoned for a crime he didn't commit (39:19–20). The story serves as yet another reminder of the powerlessness and vulnerability of enslaved women and men, as well as the silencing of their voices and the complete domination of their bodies.

## Crumbs of Comfort and Voices of Dissent

There are a few laws that attempt to mitigate the impact of enslavement. For example, Deuteronomy 15:12–14 limits the duration of debt bondage for enslaved Israelites to a maximum of six years, and it also enjoins enslavers to give generous provisions to the enslaved people they release, rather than sending them away "empty-handed." Other laws stipulate that all enslaved people (both Israelites and non-Israelites) are allowed to rest on the Sabbath and observe festivals and religious celebrations along with their Israelite enslavers (e.g., Exodus 12:44; 20:10; 23:12; Deuteronomy 5:14; 12:12; 16:11, 14).[10] And according to Exodus 21:26–27, if an enslaver strikes an enslaved person and either blinds them or knocks out a tooth, then the enslaved person is to be given their freedom as a means of compensation.

But to me, these laws feel like tiny crumbs of comfort when compared with the magnitude of structural violence that underpins enslavement. And even when we search outside the law codes for dissenting voices to this practice, we only ever hear the occasional shout,

---

10 The rationale for allowing enslaved people to observe the Sabbath is unclear—were the laws intended to ensure that enslaved people could enjoy regular rest? Did they affirm enslaved people's humanity and their full inclusion among God's holy people? Or were they more concerned with ensuring that the entire community recognized God's holiness through their obedience to these laws? Walter Brueggemann suggests that the laws set apart the Sabbath as "a day of social equalization for those who on all other days are quite unequal." If that's the case, one day out of seven is marginally better than none, but it's still not good enough. See Walter Brueggemann, "Sabbath as Alternative," *Word & World* 36, no. 3 (2016): 247–56 (citation 251).

most of which come from the prophets. Amos and Micah lambast the wealthy elites of Israel and Judah, respectively, for exploiting the system of debt bondage to oppress their impoverished brothers and sisters (Amos 2:6; 8:6; Micah 6:1–5). Jeremiah complains that the people of Jerusalem continue to enslave their fellow Hebrews despite promising to stop (Jeremiah 34:12–16). And in the book of Joel, the prophet censures the nations of Tyre and Sidon for selling the people of Judah and Jerusalem into chattel enslavement (Joel 3:6 [MT 4:6]). While none of these prophets explicitly call for an end to all enslavement (chattel and debt bondage), they do shine a light on its inherent capacity to exploit the most vulnerable members of the covenant community. It's better than nothing, I guess.

## Enslavement in the New Testament

Chattel enslavement and debt bondage were also part and parcel of life in the Roman Empire, including those regions where the New Testament texts took shape. Within this context, the texts mention enslavement without ever explicitly condemning it. They also confirm that both enslavers and enslaved people were counted among the earliest followers of Jesus and were members of the nascent church. Put differently, the acceptance or practice of enslavement does not appear to have been considered at odds with faith in Christ and baptism into the church.[11]

With this in mind, let's take a closer look at depictions of enslavement in the New Testament writings. I'll start off with some of Jesus's sayings and parables recorded in the Gospels, then I'll take a quick look at some passages known as the Household Codes. Following that, I'll move on to this chapter's case file, which focuses on some passages from the letters of the apostle Paul.

---

11 For more discussion of this topic, see Jennifer A. Glancy, *Slavery in Early Christianity*, expanded ed. (Minneapolis: Fortress, 2024).

## The Sayings and Parables of Jesus

Parables are simple stories that are typically used to teach a spiritual or moral lesson. They're a bit like a fable in that they include familiar objects, places, and scenarios from everyday life, which helps the audience better understand the parable's deeper message. Given the ubiquity of enslavement in Jesus's first-century Judean context, it's not surprising that the Gospels portray him referring to this topic in some of his parables.[12]

Sometimes, enslaved people appear in Jesus's parables as background figures who perform various tasks, such as laboring in the fields (Matthew 13:24–30), preparing meals (Luke 15:22–23), and delivering messages (Matthew 22:2–10). At other times, the theme of enslavement features more prominently. For example, in the parable of the tenant farmers (Matthew 21:33–43, Mark 12:1–11, Luke 20:9–18), a landowner sends a succession of enslaved men to collect his share of the harvest from his tenants. But on each occasion, these men are beaten or even killed by the tenants who seem reluctant to pay their dues. Eventually, the landowner sends his only son, reasoning that the tenants will surely treat *him* with more respect. But the tenants kill him too, hoping to get their hands on his inheritance. "What then will the owner of the vineyard do?" Jesus asks his audience. "He will come and destroy the tenants and give the vineyard to others" (Mark 12:9; cf. Matthew 21:40–41, Luke 20:15–16).

The parable operates as a criticism of the religious authorities of the day: they are the "wicked tenants" who have failed to recognize the authority of Jesus (the landowner's "only son"). But what interests me more is the fact that the character who represents God—the

---

12 New Testament scholars hotly debate whether these and other parables recorded in the Gospels were actually spoken by the historical figure of Jesus. But we won't concern ourselves with that thorny topic, not least because it's vast and complex. And my main interest is in how the Gospel writers *portrayed* Jesus and what words they ascribed to him.

landowner—is an enslaver himself. For Christian enslavers who heard this parable, the analogy may well have boosted their ego or affirmed the moral rightness of enslavement. But how might it have sounded to enslaved Christians? How might they have felt about the fact that the God whom they worshiped and prayed to was being likened to their own enslaver, who overworked them, or beat them, or sexually abused them?

Similar questions can also be raised about other Gospel parables, where the character of the enslaver is again intended to represent God.[13] For example, in the parable of the overseer (Matthew 24:45–51, Luke 12:42–48), an enslaved man who misbehaves when left in charge of the household will be "cut in pieces" when his enslaver returns and discovers what he's done. The audience is effectively being warned that any believer who's unprepared for Christ's return will suffer serious consequences. The version of this parable found in Luke 12 ends with the warning that the enslaved person who isn't ready and waiting to welcome their enslaver will rightly receive a "beating" (12:47–48). The parable therefore affirms that physical punishments were part and parcel of an enslaved person's experience *and* that they were often regarded as being "deserved."

As well as mentioning enslavement in his parables, Jesus of the Gospels also brings this topic up in some of his sayings and teachings. At times, he uses the word for an enslaved person (Greek: *doulos*) to refer to those who are "servants" of God.[14] Specifically, enslavement is used as a metaphor or model for what it means to be a true disciple.

---

13 I don't have space to mention all the Gospel parables that use this analogy, but readers might be interested in checking out some others, including the parable of the unforgiving "servant" (Matthew 18:23–35), the parable of the wedding banquet (Matthew 22:1–14), and the parable of the talents (Matthew 25:14–30, Luke 19:12–24).

14 We also see this use of *doulos* in other New Testament texts, including James 1:1, Jude 1:1, and Revelation 1:1. And the Hebrew term for an enslaved man (*ebed*) is at times used in a similar way in the Tanakh (e.g., 2 Kings 9:7; Isaiah 49:3; Jeremiah 7:25).

In Mark 10:44–45, for example, the term *doulos* is used to explain that a disciple's leadership must be grounded in their service to others: "Whoever wishes to become great among you must be enslaved to you," says Jesus, "and whoever wishes to be first among you must be enslaved to all. For the Son of Man came not to be served but to serve and to give his life as a ransom for many." In other words, leadership among Jesus followers involves "enslavement" in the sense that the leader must be selflessly committed to serving others; by embracing this model of leadership, Jesus's disciples are following his own example.

This association between enslavement and discipleship comes up again in Luke 17:7–10, where Jesus says to his disciples,

> Who among you would say to your enslaved man who has just come in from plowing or tending sheep in the field, "Come here at once and take your place at the table"? Would you not rather say to him, "Prepare supper for me; put on your apron and serve me while I eat and drink; later you may eat and drink"? Do you thank the enslaved man for doing what was commanded? So you also, when you have done all that you were ordered to do, say, "We are worthless enslaved people; we have done only what we ought to have done!"

The questions Jesus asks his disciples here are rhetorical. Would an enslaver invite his human chattel to sit down to dinner? Of course not. Would the enslaver tell his human chattel to serve him first before *they* can have something to eat? Too right he would. And would an enslaver ever thank his human chattel for doing what they'd been ordered to do? Don't be ridiculous.

Of all the things Jesus says about enslavement, I find this one especially disturbing. These verses effectively reinforce the idea of a social hierarchy, where the enslaver "rightfully" expects obedience and servitude from those they've enslaved, and where enslaved people must embrace and accept their subordinate position on the lowest rung of the social ladder, rather than recognizing that their placement there is deeply unjust. This saying effectively confirms that enslavement is the privilege of the powerful and the duty of the powerless. Again, I think about those enslaved Christians who may have heard this Gospel passage read out in a house church or synagogue, or who may have been copying out the text in their capacity as an enslaved scribe.[15] How would they have felt when they heard their lord and savior affirm *their own* subordination at the hands of their enslaver by using it as an ideal model of discipleship?

These various sayings and parables of Jesus echo the acceptance of enslavement in the first-century context in which the Gospels were written. But it's nothing short of a tragedy that the Gospel writers who included these traditions seem to recognize that enslavement renders its victims vulnerable to violence, yet they make no attempt to condemn it. If anything, they neutralize the brutality of enslavement by likening it to an idealized form of discipleship and service to Christ.

## The Household Codes

The Household Codes (sometimes called the Domestic Codes) are found in five epistles (or letters), four of which were written under Paul's name and one under the apostle Peter's name.[16] In a nutshell, they

---

15 According to biblical scholar Candida Moss, many scribes in the Roman Empire were actually enslaved, having been taken captive from conquered territory and put to work as notaries, transcribers, and secretaries. In Christian households, they may have been tasked with transcribing and making copies of the Gospel texts. See Candida Moss, *God's Ghostwriters: Enslaved Christians and the Making of the Bible* (New York: Little, Brown & Co., 2024).

16 The Household Codes are found in Ephesians 5:22–6:9, Colossians 3:18–4:1, 1 Timothy 2–3, 6:1–2, Titus 2:1–10, and 1 Peter 3:1–7. The letter ascribed to the apostle Peter is 1 Peter (obvs), and the other four begin with salutations from Paul. However, many New Testament scholars suspect that these letters weren't written by the apostles but by others writing in their name (such as their disciples), owing to their different style and theological leanings.

consist of instructions related to relationships within the Christian[17] household, particularly those between husband and wife, parent and child, and enslaver and enslaved. The codes are based on Greco-Roman ideals about household hierarchies and power dynamics, where certain members (husbands, parents, enslavers) were expected to hold more power than others (wives, children, enslaved people). Each code therefore instructs the household members on both sides of this power dynamic how to behave in their relationships with each other so that the hierarchy is maintained and order is preserved.

The Household Codes follow a similar pattern to each other in terms of their instructions to enslaved people: they must willingly obey and respect their enslavers; they must not "talk back to them," "steal from them" (Titus 2:9–10), or "show them disrespect" (1 Timothy 6:2), and they must also endure beatings from their enslavers, whether they are deserved or not (1 Peter 2:20). Another recurring theme within these codes is the connections made between a Christian's obedience to their enslaver and their obedience to Christ. The writer of Ephesians directs enslaved Christians to embrace their enslavement enthusiastically (6:7) and obey their enslavers "with respect and trembling, in singleness of heart, as you obey Christ" (6:5). And in Colossians, they are told that obeying their enslavers is akin to "fearing the Lord" (3:22). Meanwhile, the apostle Peter reminds enslaved Christians that they were called to this life of suffering "because Christ suffered for you, leaving you an example, that you should follow in his steps" (1 Peter 2:21).

---

17 My use of the term "Christian" when discussing these Household Codes is a little anachronistic in that, at the time these texts were written (late first century CE to early second century CE), followers of Jesus were considered part of the Jewish community. As I mentioned back in Chapter 2, "Christianity" as it would come to be known didn't exist as a faith tradition separate from Judaism until some time after the New Testament texts were composed. I use the term "Christian" in this section (and also in the case file) simply as a shorthand term for the community of Jesus followers (including both Jews and gentiles) who identified as part of the Jewish community but whose beliefs about Jesus's theological significance differed from other Jewish groups of the day.

I'm sure that many contemporary readers of these Household Codes will find them deeply troubling, not least because they equate the brutality of enslavement with obedience to God and Christ. And while a couple of the codes enjoin enslavers to treat their human chattel "justly and fairly" (Colossians 4:1) and to abstain from "threatening them" (Ephesians 6:9), they still fail to recognize the inherent barbarity of a system that relegates some people to little more than a "human tool." Once again, I wonder what enslaved Christians would have thought when they heard these texts and how *they* would have felt when they were told that their suffering was "commendable before God" (1 Peter 2:20). Did it give them a sense of hope and reassurance? Or did they wonder why *their* "enslavement" as a follower of Christ involved so much more unfreedom, pain, and brutality than that of their Christian enslavers? These Household Codes remind us that, while the New Testament writers may have insisted that *all* Christians were "enslaved" to their lord and savior, the reality was that some Christians would always be more enslaved than others.[18]

## Case File: Enslavement in Paul's Letters

The apostle Paul was active in the decades following Jesus's death, and he's most well-known for the letters he wrote to nascent churches that were springing up in the ancient Mediterranean. In a number of these letters, Paul follows Jesus's lead and uses enslavement as a metaphor for discipleship (e.g., Romans 1:1; 1 Corinthians 9:19; Galatians 1:10; 5:13). And in Galatians 3:28, he dissolves the social status of enslaved/enslaver in a theological sense when he asserts, "There is no longer Jew or Greek; *there is no longer enslaved or free*; there is no longer male

---

18 Here, I'm paraphrasing a chapter title in Marianne Bjelland Kartzow's excellent book, *The Slave Metaphor and Gendered Enslavement in Early Christian Discourse: Double Trouble Embodied* (Abingdon: Routledge, 2018), Chapter 4 (eBook).

and female, for all of you are one in Christ Jesus" (emphasis added). Paul is stressing that everyday markers of Christian identity (ethnicity/ nationality, gender, and social status) no longer matter in the context of the Christian faith, as believers are all united ("all one") through their commitment to Christ. For some biblical interpreters, this verse can sound quite liberating, as it cuts through social hierarchies to find common ground among members of the Christian community. But others accuse Paul of not going far enough, because he falls far short of condemning the practice of enslavement itself. In other words, he's talking the talk, but he ain't walking the walk.

To give Paul the chance to redeem himself, let's take a look at what he has to say about the literal practice of enslavement. Specifically, I'll take a close look at 1 Corinthians 7 and the letter to Philemon. As we'll see, the apostle tends to be a little vague when it comes to discussing this topic.

## 1 Corinthians 7

Paul's first letter to the Corinthian church addresses various questions and controversies that have arisen within the community, and in 1 Corinthians 7, Paul turns to the thorny topic of celibacy. There appears to be some debate among this church's members about whether "it is good for a man not to touch a woman" (7:1). After a bit of toing and froing, Paul concludes that being celibate is a good thing, but he knows it's not suited to everyone; so if church members feel they should get married or if they're already married, then that's fine, too (7:2–11). Married couples shouldn't get divorced to lead a life of celibacy, but if either spouse is not a Christian, then divorce is probably okay (7:12– 16). Clearly on a bit of a roll, Paul then expands on this argument to include a discussion of circumcision versus non-circumcision (7:17– 20) before finally landing on the issue of Christians who are enslaved.

Paul begins by addressing enslaved Corinthian Christians: "Were you enslaved when called? Do not be concerned about it. Even if you can gain your freedom, make the most of it" (7:21). The apostle's words here are a little "fuzzy" in terms of what they mean (no offense, Paul). His initial "Do not be concerned about it" could be read as either "Try not to worry about it, everything's going to be okay" or "Dude, suck it up." And the rest of the verse is even less clear, because the Greek literally says, "If you are able to become free, rather take advantage." But take advantage of what? The chance to be liberated from enslavement (i.e., "go for it!")? Or the current situation of enslavement (i.e., "stick with what you know")? Most contemporary Bible versions use the "go for it" option—the New International Version, for example, has "If you can gain your freedom, do so."

But if we move on to 7:24,[19] Paul seems to be recommending that currently enslaved Christians *do* stay enslaved: "In whatever condition you were called [to the faith], brothers and sisters, there remain with God." This verse sounds an awful lot like 7:20, where Paul tells Christian men not to worry about circumcision: "Let each of you remain in the condition in which you were called." That is, uncircumcised men should stay that way, and circumcised men shouldn't attempt to "remove the marks of circumcision" (7:18). The shared wording in these two verses could suggest that Paul is making a similar point to the enslaved Christians in Corinth: don't change a thing.

Paul's advice to his Corinthian audience throughout this chapter can be summed up nicely with the catchphrase "keep calm and carry on." He cautions them against making any radical changes to their lives, probably because he believes they're all living through an eschatological age, where the present world order and present reality are passing away (1 Corinthians 7:29, 31), and the dawning of a new and glorious era will soon be inaugurated with the return of Christ (1 Corinthians 15:23–24; 1 Thessalonians 4:15–16). When that day comes, the current social structures and cultural traditions (such as

---

19 The intervening verses (1 Corinthians 7:22–23) don't really help us work out what's going on, as Paul reverts to using enslavement as a metaphor for Christian faith. All Christians, he says, are effectively enslaved, because they were "bought with a price" by their lord and master, Christ (7:23).

marriage, circumcision, and enslavement) will no longer matter. In other words, Paul is telling the Corinthians not to worry, because everything's about to change—and for the better.

It's hard to know how much of a comfort this message would have been to enslaved Christians in Corinth and other parts of the Roman Empire. Perhaps it *did* give them some hope, and if so, I'm glad. But I'm also aware that Paul's much anticipated "passing away" of the current age didn't transpire, and a great number of Christians (and non-Christians, too) remained enslaved and oppressed for many, many centuries to come.

## Philemon

The second text from Paul that I want to focus on in this case file is his letter to Philemon. This is Paul's shortest letter—comprising just one chapter—and he appears to have written it when he was in prison or under house arrest (Philemon 1:9). The main recipient, Philemon, is the leader of a house church (possibly in the city of Colossae),[20] and Paul is writing to him about an enslaved man called Onesimus (whose name literally means "useful"). So far so good, but exactly what Paul is saying about Onesimus and exactly what he's asking Philemon to do about Onesimus is very hard to work out.

It seems as though Philemon is Onesimus's enslaver, but for some unknown reason, Onesimus has been with Paul for "a while" (1:15–16). It's unclear how Paul and Onesimus met—did Onesimus search the apostle out, or was their meeting by happenstance? Did Philemon perhaps send him to minister to Paul while he was imprisoned, or, as many biblical scholars believe, did Onesimus run away from his enslaver and somehow encounter Paul on his travels? If he is indeed a runaway, he'd be in serious trouble—enslaved people who absconded from their enslavers could face beatings or even death (sometimes by crucifixion) if

---

20 Colossae was located in the southern region of Anatolia (modern-day Turkey).

they were caught. Anyone who harbored a runaway could also face consequences, as this practice was illegal under Roman imperial law, and it might explain why Paul feels obliged to send Onesimus back (1:12).

It sounds as though Paul is asking Philemon to treat Onesimus leniently on his return (1:17) or even to release him from enslavement so that Philemon can "have him back forever, no longer as an enslaved man but more than an enslaved man, as a beloved brother … both in the flesh and in the Lord" (1:15–16). Paul may also be asking (in a very roundabout way) if Onesimus can stay on with him, whether enslaved or free. "I would have been glad to keep him with me," writes Paul, "in order that he might serve me on your behalf during my imprisonment for the gospel, but I preferred to do nothing without your consent in order that your goodness might not be by compulsion but of your own accord" (1:13–14). In other words, Paul *could* be saying, "I'd really like him to stay and help me, but obviously, it's your decision because you're his enslaver." The apostle even offers to pay for anything Onesimus owes to Philemon, which could suggest Onesimus is enslaved to Philemon through debt bondage.

Whatever the context of this intriguing letter, one thing stands out for me above all else. The person at its center—Onesimus—is the only one whose needs and wishes aren't taken into account. Paul is writing to Philemon to discuss the fate of this man. Where should he go? How should he be treated? Whom should he serve? At no point does Paul raise the issue of what *Onesimus* wants; this speaks to Onesimus's status as an enslaved man—a "living tool"—whose value is measured (as his name suggests) according to his "usefulness." His fate is being determined by an apostle who speaks of Christian brotherhood but who never explicitly invites his enslaved "brother" to join this discussion. As theologian Matthew Johnson argues, "Unless and until Onesimus has an equal voice in the conversation, so to speak, he will not have even the potential to be a brother."[21]

---

21 Matthew V. Johnson, "Onesimus Speaks: Diagnosing the Hys/Terror of the Text," in *Onesimus Our Brother: Reading Religion, Race, and Culture*

### Case Closed … for Now

If I've sounded unduly critical of Paul throughout this case file, then I make no apology (except to you, dear readers, if I offend). To be sure, the apostle lived in an empire where enslavement was considered as natural as breathing; nevertheless, he was a deeply intelligent man, so I find it hard to believe that he didn't recognize the brutality of a system that treated his enslaved brothers and sisters in Christ as dehumanized chattel. As the writer of many a scorching letter, Paul is famous for not holding back when it comes to getting things off his chest or speaking home truths; so the fact that he gets very reticent and tongue-tied when it comes to the topic of enslavement (both in 1 Corinthians 7 and Philemon) is disappointing to say the least. Had it been otherwise, I'm confident that the apostle could have achieved great things.

## Closing Thoughts

Enslavement is far from a thing of the ancient past. Many readers will live in countries marked by the shadows of enslavement that have stretched across our world for centuries, if not millennia And according to a report published in 2022, around fifty million people are currently enslaved, through either debt bondage, chattel enslavement, forced labor, forced pregnancy, or forced marriage.[22] That, my friends, is a sobering thought indeed. To be sure, enslavement that occurs in our contemporary contexts takes different forms than it did back in the biblical periods, not least because it is now outlawed in many if not most parts of the world. But the same forms of structural violence that rendered some people vulnerable to enslavement in ancient Southwest

---

*in Philemon*, ed. Matthew V. Johnson, James A. Noel, and Demetrius K. Williams (Minneapolis: Fortress, 2012), 91–100 (96).
22 Anti-Slavery, "What is Modern Slavery?" https://www.antislavery.org/slavery-today/modern-slavery/, accessed July 4, 2024.

Asia and the Roman Empire (social inequality, misogyny, ethnic preju-
dice) continue to sustain it today. In other words, the enslavement we
read about in the Tanakh and New Testament has a living legacy in our
histories and communities that we can't afford to ignore.

# CHAPTER SIX

# Human Sacrifice

Human sacrifice—particularly the sacrifice of children—is a horrible topic to talk about, but this is a book about violence in the Bible, so I couldn't in good conscience leave it out. Because, like the proverbial elephant in the room, it's right there before our eyes, and we can't afford to ignore it.

To begin making sense of human sacrifice, we need to understand the significance of sacrifices more generally. Throughout history, sacrificial rituals have played a role in many religious traditions, and they often involve the slaughter of an animal (usually on an altar) as an offering to a deity. Sacrifices have often been understood as a way to build relationships with the divine realm—think of them as gifts to the gods, if you like, which allow the person making the sacrifice to give thanks to a deity or deities for blessings received, or to request divine assistance in times of trouble, or to ask for forgiveness after doing something wrong.

In ancient Southwest Asia and the Roman Empire (home to the Tanakh and New Testament, respectively), the religious sacrifice of other-than-human animals (such as goats, bulls, rams, lambs, and doves) appears to have been commonplace. A number of texts in the Tanakh describe this form of ritualized killing, which often included the burning of all or part of the animal as an offering to God (e.g., Genesis 8:20; Leviticus 7–9; 1 Samuel 13:8–10). The Hebrew term for "burnt offering" is *olah* (from the verb *alah*, meaning "to ascend"), and it captures the belief that the savory smoke from the offering rose towards the heavens, where it was smelt and appreciated by God (e.g., Genesis 8:21; Leviticus 1:9; Numbers 18:17).

But other-than-human animals are not the only victims of sacrifice mentioned in the Bible. In a number of texts, the topic of *human* sacrifice is raised, either explicitly or implicitly. On some occasions, this practice seems to serve the same purpose as other animal sacrifices—they're intended to please a deity, request divine aid, or make atonement for sin. But at other times, their meaning isn't quite so clear.

Now, we'll never know for sure whether the human sacrifices described in the Bible actually took place in historical terms, but that's not my main concern here. What *does* interest me is the way they're described and the meanings that they're given. For some contemporary readers, the idea that such an extraordinary form of violence is entertained at all in the Bible can be shocking and confronting. So my task in this chapter is to examine the biblical evidence and discover how this practice was understood in the biblical worlds of the Tanakh and New Testament. I'll begin with the Tanakh—including our case file on Jephthah's daughter in Judges 11—before turning to New Testament understandings of sacrifice in relation to Jesus's crucifixion.


## Human Sacrifice in the Tanakh

Archaeological evidence suggests that human sacrifice may have been practiced in certain regions of ancient Southwest Asia for thousands of years before the Common Era. And according to various texts in the Tanakh, it might have been part of religious life in Israel and the surrounding nations. Some of these texts condemn it as an idolatrous non-Israelite practice that's abhorred by Israel's god, but others give us the impression it's an effective and acceptable religious ritual used in Israel and beyond.

## But It Works! The "Efficacy" of Human Sacrifice

The first text I want to look at is 2 Kings 3, which presents human sacrifice as something practiced by other nations in times of crisis. At the start of this narrative, Israel is at war with the neighboring land of Moab. The Israelites have the upper hand and are sweeping through Moab, destroying cities and ruining the land (3:24–25). When they reach the city of Kirhareseth, King Mesha of Moab realizes he's about to lose the battle, so he takes his firstborn son (who was to succeed him as king) and sacrifices him as a burnt offering on the wall of the city. As a result, "A great wrath came against Israel," and the Israelite troops immediately withdrew and returned to their own land, leaving Kirhareseth undefeated (3:27).

This story is disturbing and fascinating in equal measure, not least because it seems to portray the efficacy of human sacrifice. King Mesha is on the brink of losing the battle *until* he sacrifices his firstborn son in a last-ditch attempt to save his people and his land (as well as himself). The offering is presumably made to Moab's national deity, Chemosh, and we can suppose that it's Chemosh's "great wrath" that scares off the Israelite army (and presumably Israel's god, too). This deity is clearly pleased with the sacrifice, so he reciprocates by helping King Mesha out of a very tight corner. The narrator of this story expresses neither horror at Mesha's actions nor surprise at the outcome of the sacrifice. The fact that it "works" only confirms that human sacrifices made during battle were understood as a way to effectively petition a national god for urgent assistance.

## Keeping Up with the Neighbors

Mesha's sacrifice of his son takes place in Moab, but there are plenty of texts that hint this practice also occurred in Israel and Judah. On some occasions, it's roundly condemned, and the Israelites are accused of adopting this bad habit from their neighbors. In other words, human sacrifice is presented as a "foreign" practice that has no place whatsoever among the covenant community.

The texts that appear to condemn human sacrifice refer to this practice in a variety of ways. The prophet Isaiah pulls no punches when he decries those Israelites who "slaughter [their] children in the valleys, under the clefts of the rocks" (Isaiah 57.4–5), while Ezekiel mentions twice that the people of Jerusalem have "slaughtered" their children and offered them up to be "devoured" as "food" for false gods and idols (Ezekiel 16:20–21; 23:37–39). Other texts accuse the Israelites of copying their neighbors' idolatrous practices by "burning" their sons and daughters "in the fire" or making their children "pass through the fire" for the benefit of a god or gods. For example, Deuteronomy 12:29–31 accuses the Canaanite people of "burn[ing] their sons and their daughters in the fire to their gods" (cf. Deuteronomy 18:10). And in Psalm 106, the psalmist confesses that the Israelites began to do likewise: "They sacrificed their sons and their daughters to the demons; they poured out innocent blood, the blood of their sons and daughters, whom they sacrificed to the idols of Canaan, and the land was polluted with blood" (106:37–38). This appears to be confirmed in 2 Kings, where we're told that some of the Israelites, including Judean kings Ahaz and Manasseh, made their children "pass through fire" (16:2–3; 17:17; 21:6).

One of the fiercest critics of human sacrifice is the prophet Jeremiah, who accuses the people of Jerusalem on more than one occasion of building shrines "to burn their children in the fire as burnt offerings to Baal" (Jeremiah 19:5; 32:35). These offerings appear to take place at a location called "Topheth" in "the valley of the son of Hinnom" (7:31; 19:6; 32:35), which was likely located either in or near the city of Jerusalem.[1] Jeremiah refers to Topeth as the "valley of slaughter," and he insists to his audience that God has *never* commanded, decreed,

1 The valley of the son of Hinnom is sometimes referred to by its slightly shorter title "valley of Hinnom" (Hebrew: *ge-hinnom*), which literally means "valley of lamentation" (e.g., Joshua 15:8). The same term is used in the New Testament (Greek: *gehenna*) to refer to a place where sinners will be subjected to a fiery punishment from God (e.g., Matthew 5:29–30; Mark 9:43; James

or even thought about the sacrifice of children (7:31; 19:5; 32:35). In other words, if Israelite children are being sacrificed as burnt offerings, then it's *not* at the behest of Israel's deity.

Another interesting point to note about Jeremiah 32:35 is that the prophet mentions children being sacrificed "to Molek." The name Molek also crops up in the law codes of Leviticus, which warn the Israelites that those who "give their offspring to Molek shall be put to death" (Leviticus 20:2; also 18:21). Now, the exact identity of Molek has long been the subject of debate among biblical scholars. Many believe it's the name of a deity whom the Israelites started to follow under the influence of their near neighbors. But others have suggested that it's the technical term given to a religious ritual involving human sacrifice. In other words, people who "give their offspring to Molek" are performing a Molek ritual, which involves offering up their children as burnt offerings. If we go with this second interpretation, we're left with the possibility that the Israelites may have been making "Molek" sacrifices to different gods, *including* the god of Israel, in the belief that it was an acceptable form of worship. This could explain Jeremiah's repeated and insistent claims that such a practice was *in no way* commanded by God (Jeremiah 7:31; 19:5; 32:35).

Despite Jeremiah's protests, there are two texts that appear to suggest human/child sacrifice could, in certain circumstances, be an acceptable way of relating to Israel's god—Genesis 22 (the near sacrifice of Isaac) and Judges 11 (the actual sacrifice of Jephthah's unnamed daughter—our case file). Let's look at each of these in turn.

## A Near Miss: Genesis 22

In Genesis 22, God decides to "test" the patriarch Abraham. The deity tells him, "Take your son, your only son Isaac, whom you love, and go to the land of Moriah and offer him there as a burnt offering on one of

---

3:6). In some English versions of the New Testament (e.g., NRSVue, King James Version, New International Version), *gehenna* is translated as "hell."

the mountains that I shall show you" (22:2). It's unclear why Abraham is being tested in this way. Has he done something to make God question his faith and obedience? Or is this some sort of punishment for a wrongdoing he's committed? Whatever the reason, Abraham does as he's told. Without so much as a murmur of dissent,[2] he sets out with Isaac to the land of Moriah. When they arrive, Abraham "built an altar and laid the wood in order. He bound his son Isaac and laid him on the altar on top of the wood. Then Abraham reached out his hand and took the knife to kill his son" (22:9–10). But just at that moment, an angel of the LORD calls from the heavens and says, "Do not lay your hand on the boy or do anything to him, for now I know that you fear God, since you have not withheld your son, your only son, from me" (22:12). Then Abraham spots a ram caught by its horns in a nearby bush, so he sacrifices that instead of Isaac. The angel goes on to deliver a divine blessing to Abraham, which he apparently deserves "because you have done this, and have not withheld your son, your only son" (22:16).

The narrative of Genesis 22 raises so many questions that I don't have space to go into here; but let me summarize a few things we can take away from this text of terror. First of all, God is depicted as a deity who not only demands the murder and burning of a child but also rewards the child's father for being prepared to kill his own son in this way. Regardless of the fact that the sacrifice never happens, this is still a staggering portrayal of God, which speaks once again to the Israelites' belief that, for better *and* for worse, their deity's limitless capacity for love and mercy is matched by an aptitude for violence and a desire for power and control.

Second and related to this, Genesis 22 shows us so clearly the hierarchy of power involved in the practice of human sacrifice. At the top of this hierarchy sits the deity, who can demand or expect such a sacrifice. The person making the sacrifice (Abraham in this case) is situated

---

2 Abraham's seeming acquiescence here is strange, especially given his actions in Genesis 18:22–33 where he argues at length with God in an effort to prevent the deity from destroying the city of Sodom and its inhabitants.

lower in the hierarchy and feels obligated to make the sacrifice, either in an effort to please the deity or because they fear the consequences were they to refuse. At the bottom of this hierarchy sits the victim of the sacrifice (here, it's Isaac), who has no capacity to refuse their role because they are not as powerful as either the sacrifice-maker or the deity who demands it. So perhaps we can think of human sacrifice as a form of structural violence, where those who are deprived of power are more likely to be victimized, and those with greater power than them reap the benefits of their victimization. Isaac is nearly killed; Abraham is blessed; and God is rewarded with the knowledge that loyal followers are prepared to obey even the most outrageous divine demands.

Lastly, I've always wondered what Isaac was thinking during this entire event. Did he work out what his dad was planning? Did he remonstrate or struggle, and is that why Abraham had to bind him on the altar? I also wonder about his relationship with his dad after they left Moriah and headed back home. Would he ever trust Abraham again? Interestingly enough, the Genesis narrative never records any further speech or interactions between father and son; even when Abraham arranges Isaac's marriage to Rebekah (Genesis 24), the two never appear to meet or speak to each other. So while Abraham didn't go through with the actual sacrifice of Isaac, I suspect that what this father *did* sacrifice was his relationship with his son.

If Isaac managed to escape his fate as a sacrificial offering, then Jephthah's unnamed daughter isn't nearly so fortunate. Let's turn to our case file so we can learn more about her.

## Case File: Judges 11

### The Vow

Judges 11 begins by introducing us to Jephthah, a "mighty" Israelite warrior (11:1) who has been charged with leading the battle against the Ammonite people. As he prepares for the fight ahead, we're told the "spirit of the LORD" comes upon him, and he makes a vow to God: "If you will give the Ammonites into my hand, then whatever comes out of the doors of my house to meet me, when I return victorious from the Ammonites, shall be the LORD's, to be offered up by me as a burnt offering" (11:30–31). The Hebrew word translated as "whatever" (*asher*) can also mean "whoever." So it's unclear if Jephthah is imagining a human or other-than-human animal as the object of the sacrifice—the vow leaves open the possibility it could be either. In any case, God clearly decides to accept this vow because the next thing we're told is that the deity has enabled Jephthah to inflict a "mighty defeat" against the Ammonites and thus secure Israel's victory (11:32–33).

So far so good. But after the battle, things go decidedly pear-shaped for Jephthah. God has kept his side of the bargain, so Jephthah now has to fulfill his promise to sacrifice whoever or whatever comes out to greet him on his return. And horror of horrors, who does he see when he reaches home but his only daughter, "coming out to meet him with timbrels and with dancing" (11:34).[3] Jephthah is understandably distraught when he sees her. He tears his garments (an Israelite sign of mourning) and says, "Alas, my daughter! You have brought me very low; you have become the cause of great trouble to me. For I have opened my mouth to the Lord, and I cannot take back my vow" (11:35).

There are a couple of things to note here. First, Jephthah's words seem more than a little harsh—he sounds as though he's blaming his daughter for the mess that his own vow has put him in. But I'm prepared to let this slide (to an extent)—I'm sure we've all said things we regret when we're caught up in terrible events. But the more important point I want to make relates to Jephthah's belief that he can't "take back" his vow. To be sure, vows, oaths, and curses were a serious business in ancient Southwest Asia—they were typically regarded as binding promises, especially when the deity was petitioned in the process.

---

3 We're never told the name of Jephthah's daughter or how old she is. But as she's unmarried and still living in her father's house, we can presume she's fairly young—a tween or teen at most.

Jephthah has effectively told God, "If you do X, then I promise I'll do Y." God made good on the X, so Jephthah must now keep *his* side of the bargain and deliver the Y.

At the same time, though, there are some texts that suggest it's possible to wiggle out of a rashly made promise without any serious repercussions. For example, later in the book of Judges, a woman curses (swears an oath against) whichever jerk has stolen her life savings.[4] But when her son Micah 'fesses up that he's the jerk in question, she blesses him instead (as a way to nullify the curse), and he gives her back the money (17:1–3). And in 1 Samuel 14:24, King Saul curses any of his soldiers who eat food before nightfall.[5] When he learns his son Jonathan has scoffed down some honey, Saul tells him he's going to have to kill him to fulfill the curse. Thankfully, Jonathan's fellow soldiers object, and he ends up being spared, possibly by being swapped (or "ransomed") for an other-than-human animal offering (14:44–45). Both of these stories suggest that oaths, curses, and vows didn't necessarily need to be fulfilled to the letter—there *were* ways around them. So Jephthah's insistence that he couldn't take back his vow remains a bit of a mystery, especially given what's at stake. And we're left in no doubt that he did carry through with his side of the bargain—as the narrator tells us, he sacrificed his daughter "according to the vow he had made" (Judges 11:39).

### Virginity and Sacrifice

Unlike the silent Isaac, Jephthah's daughter gets to speak when she first learns about her father's plans. Yet her response is uncannily measured

---

4 Such an oath or curse would involve the person saying something like "may the deity do X to whoever did/does this terrible thing," where X involves a divine punishment of sorts.

5 Why Saul does this is anyone's guess—the soldiers are busy fighting the Philistines, so they're bound to be famished. The narrator puts in their two cents worth when they describe Saul's curse as "a very rash act" (1 Samuel 14:24).

and calm:[6] "My father, if you have opened your mouth to the LORD, do to me according to what has gone out of your mouth, now that the LORD has given you vengeance against your enemies, the Ammonites" (11:36). Then she follows this up with a request: "Let this thing be done for me: grant me two months, so that I may go and wander on the mountains and bewail my virginity, my companions and I" (11:37). This seems such a strange thing to ask—of all the reasons she might bewail dying so young (and in such a horrific way), why does she want to mourn her virginity? Some scholars suggest she's lamenting that she'll never get to be a wife or a mother—two social roles to which biblical women were expected to aspire. If that's the case, I suspect she's being portrayed as the "ideal" daughter here—obedient to her father, sexually "pure," regretful about her thwarted plans to enjoy marriage and motherhood, and a completely "willing" sacrifice who recognizes the importance of keeping promises to God. In other words, she's humbly accepting her lower position in the hierarchy of power, which requires her to consent to the demands of her more powerful father and an even more powerful deity. Portrayed as such an obliging and idealized virgin sacrifice, she becomes an acceptable offering to God.

Jephthah's daughter departs for two months, and on her return, her father fulfills his vow and sacrifices her to God as a burnt offering.[7] The narrator tells us rather awkwardly that, at the time of her death, "She had never slept with a man," as though that were the most tragic feature of this truly awful story (11:39). It may also be a way of reassuring readers that her sexual status hadn't changed during her two-month absence—she remained a sexually "pure" virgin at the time of her death.

Judges 11 ends with the narrator telling us about an Israelite custom that arose following the girl's death: "For four days every year the daughters of Israel would go out to lament the daughter of Jephthah

---

6 I'd have been raging, I can tell you.
7 I always feel so sad that she didn't just run away with her friends during her two-month absence.

the Gileadite" (11:39–40). In other words, Israelite girls and women found a way to memorialize Jephthah's daughter so that she wouldn't be forgotten. The text doesn't go into detail about what happens during this four-day event, but I'd like to think the participants spent their time plotting the downfall of the sacrificial system that had stolen the life of their sister.

### Case Closed…for Now

The story of Jephthah's daughter has, at times, been read as a cautionary tale against the evils of human sacrifice. But any critique of this practice is hard to detect in the narrative. To be sure, Jephthah suffers the loss of his only daughter, but at the same time, readers are reminded that vows involving human sacrifices actually do work. As with King Mesha of Moab (2 Kings 3:27), Jephthah wins his war because he promises his deity a burnt offering, and his deity accepts this offer. The possibility that this offering would involve the slaughter of a human being deters neither Jephthah nor God from entering into this deal, and both parties end up keeping their side of the bargain. Also, as with Abraham, Jephthah is rewarded for his willingness to make such a sacrifice—after all, God grants him a "massive defeat" of the Ammonites, thereby boosting his honor and status as a mighty warrior (Judges 11:33). Unlike Abraham, though, God doesn't step in at the last minute to prevent Jephthah from killing his daughter, which suggests that, in this case at least, the deity gladly accepted a human victim (a child, no less) as a burnt offering.

## The Sacrificial Lamb

The story told in Judges 11 has certain points of similarity with the New Testament accounts of Jesus's crucifixion. Theologians over the centuries have argued that, just like Jephthah's daughter, Jesus willingly offered himself as a sacrifice to God so that those he left behind gained some benefit, or divine blessing, as the result of his death. To be sure, Jesus wasn't killed on a sacrificial altar during a religious ritual—he was crucified by the Roman authorities as punishment for what they perceived to be his dangerous claims to power. So his murder was purely political, rather than religious. But during the years after the crucifixion, Jesus's early followers looked for ways to give theological meaning to his execution. One of the ways they did this—among others—was to draw on the idea of sacrifice. They began to understand Jesus's death as a voluntary sacrifice offered *by* God and *to* God that bestowed blessings on God's followers and atoned (made amends) for their sins.

The idea that sacrifices could achieve the forgiveness of sins would have been familiar to both Jewish and gentile audiences during the first century CE when the New Testament texts were being written. The law codes in the Tanakh lay out a series of guidelines for "sin offerings," where the guilty party gives the temple priest an other-than-human animal, such as a sheep or goat, which is then offered up as a burnt offering to "make atonement" and seek forgiveness for the sin that has been committed.[8] Similar "piacular" (reparatory) offerings were also commonly practiced in Roman religions during this period, and animals would be sacrificed to seek divine forgiveness for wrongdoings.

It's within this context, then, that some New Testament writers made sense of Jesus's crucifixion and death as a form of "sin offering" or atoning sacrifice. For example, the apostle Paul argues that Jesus's death offers redemption to sinners because God "put [him] forward as a sacrifice of atonement by his blood, effective through faith" (Romans 3:25). Using similar language to Paul, the author of 1 John explains that God sent his son to be "the atoning sacrifice for our sins, and not for ours only but also for the sins of the whole world" (1 John 2:2; 4:10).

As well as viewing Jesus's death as an atoning sacrifice, the apostle Paul also relates it to the Passover traditions when he refers to Jesus as "the paschal lamb" who "has been sacrificed" through his crucifixion

---

8 The rules and regulations around sin offerings are laid out in detail in Leviticus 5–7.

(1 Corinthians 5:7). The paschal lamb is not a sin offering per se but refers to the lamb that was once sacrificed at the Jewish festival of Passover, which commemorates the Israelites' exodus from Egypt. Exodus 12 recounts that the blood from this lamb was daubed on the doorframes of Israelites' houses in Egypt as a sign for God to "pass over" their homes and spare them the final plague that was inflicted on the Egyptians—the killing of firstborn humans and livestock (12:7, 12–13). So by referring to Jesus as the paschal lamb, Paul appears to understand his death as a sacrifice that offers believers redemption and salvation from death. The Gospel of John also draws on this idea of Jesus as a sacrificial lamb in its opening chapter, where John the Baptist twice describes Jesus as "the Lamb of God who takes away the sin of the world" (John 1:29, 36).

The idea that Jesus's death was a sacrifice raises an interesting question: was he a *willing* sacrifice in the same way that Jephthah's daughter appeared to be? Well, the Gospel traditions suggest that Jesus was aware of his sacrificial role, but they also make clear he recognized the enormity of what it entailed. Crucifixion was a horrific method of public torture and execution, which was prolonged, excruciating, and deeply shameful for the victim.[9] Growing up in Roman-occupied Palestine, Jesus may well have known this and could have dreaded the ordeal that lay ahead of him. This seems to be acknowledged in the scene that takes place shortly before his arrest, which is recounted in the Gospels of Matthew, Mark, and Luke. Jesus goes with some of his disciples to the garden of Gethsemane, which is located at the foot of the Mount of Olives in East Jerusalem. He's feeling agitated and deeply distressed, we are told, so he takes himself off to a quiet corner of the garden and says a prayer to God: "My father, if it is possible, let this cup pass from me, yet not what I want but what you want" (Matthew 26:39, cf. Mark

---

9 For more information about Roman crucifixion, see David Tombs, "Crucifixion, State Terror, and Sexual Abuse," *Union Seminary Quarterly Review* 53 (1999): 89–109, https://doi.org/10.7916/d8-wypm-vt48 (open access).

14:36, Luke 22:42). In Matthew and Mark, Jesus repeats this prayer a short time later (Matthew 26:42, Mark 14:39), and in Matthew 26:44, he says it a third time. Luke's Gospel states that, after Jesus said this prayer, an angel appeared to him and gave him strength, but "in his anguish he prayed more earnestly, and his sweat became like great drops of blood falling down on the ground" (Luke 22:43–44).

This is such a heartbreaking scene, which captures Jesus's intense fear and grief at his impending execution on an imperial Roman cross. He knows that this is what God wants—or needs—him to do, and like Jephthah's daughter, he *is* prepared to go through with it if that is God's will. But unlike Jephthah's daughter, he isn't portrayed as accepting his fate with an unnatural calmness or resignation. He does not *want* to accept this "cup" of suffering from God, but he will not refuse to take it unless God his father tells him otherwise. So yes, Jesus is an obedient and voluntary sacrifice, but I'm not sure he embraces this role with any alacrity or enthusiasm. This in no way detracts from the significance of his passion and crucifixion—if anything, the *un*willingness that he expresses in his prayers at Gethsemane makes his own personal sacrifice all the more profound.

## Closing Thoughts

The biblical texts unequivocally describe the violence of human sacrifice. At times, this practice is heavily condemned, while at other times, it appears to occur with the divine seal of approval. This seeming contradiction isn't terribly surprising—after all, the texts of the Tanakh and New Testament were composed over many hundreds of years, and these changing views on human sacrifice may reflect new theological and cultural understandings that arose within the biblical faith communities during this time.

It's hard to know what to do with these texts when we look at them today. We could shake our heads and be grateful that the religious sacrifice of human beings is now *exceedingly* rare and is outlawed in most (if not all) countries around the world. But that response feels a bit inadequate, because there are still so many other forms of violence perpetrated within religious communities today, which, although not "sacrificial" in a theological sense, still rely on the same hierarchy of power that underpinned the ancient practices of human sacrifice. I'm thinking particularly of the violence of exclusion and intolerance that's all too often targeted against people of other faiths and those who do not subscribe to a religious faith; and against queer and transgender people; and against people whose ethnicity, skin color, or social class is treated as a sign they "don't belong." I'm also thinking about the shameful legacy of sexual abuse that has long been hidden and silenced within so many faith communities. The victims of all these forms of violence are not literally "sacrificed," but like Isaac and Jephthah's daughter, they *are* disempowered and rendered vulnerable for the benefit of those more powerful than them. So when we read about human sacrifice in the biblical texts, perhaps we should imitate the girls who continued to commemorate Jephthah's daughter and, like them, refuse to let these victims' names and memories be forgotten.

# So What?

We've reached the end of our journey, and now it's time for me to leave you with a few parting words before we all head home. I hope you've found our travels through the world of biblical violence an enriching experience, and I also hope it wasn't too hard-going. For my part, it's been an absolute privilege serving as your guide and travel companion.

My aim for this book has been to illustrate the ways that biblical texts of terror carry a great deal of significance, both for their ancient audiences and for Bible readers in more recent history and up to the present day. As I said way back in the Infomercial, these texts can shine a light on topics that make many of us feel uneasy—such as fear, pain, danger, grief, injustice, and death—but they let us think about such topics from a safer distance. They disclose the ways that violence can spiral and reverberate across generations, shattering the fragile bonds of human community and connection. They uncover ancient understandings of the multifaceted (and sometimes troublingly violent) nature of God and the divine realm. They illuminate how inequalities of power can allow violence to thrive in plain sight. And they remind us that our very human, everyday emotions—such as anger, jealousy, and shame—so often lie at the heart of violent words, thoughts, and actions.

More than that, though, I hope it's become clear as you've read this book that the Bible's texts of terror leave a significant legacy that stretches across space and time and remains with us today. This is a legacy of beliefs, values, and language that can, at times, scaffold and sustain various forms of structural violence, including misogyny, enslavement, ethnic supremacy, religious intolerance, and male privilege and power. Located within the pages of a sacred book that still carries a lot of religious and cultural freight, these beliefs and values (and the language that articulates them) have a considerable capacity to shape readers' understandings of the world and their relationships with others. As I've mentioned on more than one occasion throughout the previous chapters, the Bible's texts of terror often reflect and reinforce the same attitudes (about gender, race, sexuality, religion, and social status) that have perpetuated (and continue to perpetuate) various forms of violence and injustice, particularly against those who are forced to occupy the lower rungs of the social ladder.

As Bible readers, we are all recipients of this enduring legacy of biblical violence, and it's up to us what we do with it. Should we ignore it? Pretend it's not there? Pass it on to someone else? Or do we unwrap it, hold it up to the light, and search for its potential to inspire or justify further violence? What *you* choose to do, dear readers, is entirely up to you, but let me leave you with a metaphor from Isabel Wilkerson's powerful book *Caste: The Origins of Our Discontent*, which I think offers a fitting response to this legacy and the violence it helps sustain.

Wilkerson draws on the image of an old house to talk about the structural violence that has long beset her American homeland.[1] Old houses, she says, need never-ending maintenance to keep them structurally sound and safe. The owners who've inherited these houses can't afford to ignore the leaks, cracks, and sinking foundations because these problems never go away on their own—they only get worse. Despite this, some maintenance-shy owners may attempt to live with the inconveniences caused by such issues—they'll try to ignore the fact that the floors are starting to slope, they'll put down buckets to catch the rain when it drips through the leaky roof, and they'll keep plastering over the cracks in the walls each time they reappear. Eventually, the owners won't even *notice* that they're living in a house that's slowly crumbling around them. To be sure, these longstanding problems aren't

---

1 Wilkerson, *Caste*, 15–16.

their fault—they weren't even born when the house was built. But it *is* their inheritance, so it's up to them to look after it now. Because if they don't have the courage to confront these problems, the foundations will keep sinking, the cracks will only get bigger, and the buckets to catch the rainwater will eventually overflow.

When I first read this passage in Wilkerson's book, it struck me that the Bible is also an "old house" that many of us have inherited, either through our faith or as part of our cultural heritage. Its texts of terror—which have long endorsed and helped perpetuate various forms of violence—are the fissures in the foundations, the leaky roof, and the cracked supporting walls. We can't simply get rid of them or make do without them, because they're an integral part of the house. But we can't afford to ignore them either, because they'll inevitably become an even greater hazard for the house's inhabitants and all those who visit.

So what should we do? As caretakers of this "old house," it's up to us to confront its texts of terror before they can do further harm. And the best way we can caretake is by continuing the work I've outlined in this book—we shine a light on these texts in order to explore the source of their violence; we identify and diagnose the dangers that they pose; and we work out ways to reduce their capacity to foster further violence in our communities and our world. Then, slowly but surely, we can begin the repairs that keep this old house a warmer and safer place for the residents who live in it, the people who drop by, and its neighbors, near and far.

So let's head back to the house. There's still a lot of work to do.

# Things for Normal People to Read (Or Not ... No Judgment)

## General Resources on Violence in the Bible

Blyth, Caroline, and Emily Colgan. *The Bloody Bible*. Produced by Caroline Blyth, Emily Colgan, and Richard Bonifant. 2022–2024. Podcast. https://www.bloodybiblepodcast.com/

Collins, John J. *What are Biblical Values? What the Bible Says on Key Ethical Issues*. New Haven: Yale University Press, 2019.

## Murder

Gaines, Janet Howe. "How Bad Was Jezebel?" *Biblical History Daily*, April 1, 2023. https://www.biblicalarchaeology.org/daily/people-cultures-in-the-bible/people-in-the-bible/how-bad-was-jezebel/.

Ornstein, Dan. *Cain v. Abel: A Jewish Courtroom Drama*. Lincoln, PA: University of Nebraska Press; Jewish Publication Society, 2020.

## Divine Violence

Crossan, John Dominic. *How to Read the Bible and Still Be a Christian: Struggling with Divine Violence from Genesis Through Revelation.* San Francisco: HarperOne, 2015.

Hamori, Esther J. *God's Monsters: Vengeful Spirits, Deadly Angels, Hybrid Creatures, and Divine Hitmen of the Bible.* Minneapolis: Broadleaf Books, 2023.

Stavrakopoulou, Francesca. *God: An Anatomy.* London: Picador, 2021.


## Gender-Based Violence

Dawson, Rosie. *The Shiloh Podcast.* Produced by Rosie Dawson. 2020–2024. Podcast. https://podcasts.apple.com/gb/podcast/the-shiloh-podcast/id1517019190

Melanchthon, Monica Jyotsna, and Robyn J. Whitaker, *Terror in the Bible: Rhetoric, Gender, and Violence.* Atlanta: SBL Press, 2021. Open access: https://www.sbl-site.org/assets/pdfs/pubs/9781628375008_OA.pdf

Trible, Phyllis. *Texts of Terror: Literary-Feminist Readings of Biblical Narratives.* 40th Anniversary Ed. Minneapolis: Fortress, 2022.


## Child Sacrifice

Levinson, Jon D. *The Death and Resurrection of the Beloved Son: The Transformation of Child Sacrifice in Judaism and Christianity.* New Haven: Yale University Press, 1993.

Monroe, Lauren A. S. "Disembodied Women: Sacrificial Language and the Deaths of Bat-Jephthah, Cozbi, and the Bethlehemite Concubine." *Catholic Biblical Quarterly* 75 (2013): 32–52.

## Enslavement

Glancy, Jennifer A. *Slavery in Early Christianity: Expanded Edition.* Minneapolis: Fortress, 2024.

Kartzow, Marianne Bjelland. *The Slave Metaphor and Gendered Enslavement in Early Christian Discourse: Double Trouble Embodied.* Abingdon: Routledge, 2018.

Lucas, Philippa. "Relating Genesis 16 to Sexual Abuse in the Church: Hagar as a Biblical Parallel." *Anglican Theological Review*, 105, no. 1 (2023): 87–96. Open access: https://doi.org/10.1177/00033286221141858.

## Structural Violence

Wilkerson, Isabel. *Caste: The Origins of Our Discontent.* New York: Random House, 2023.

# About the Author

Caroline Blyth (PhD University of Edinburgh) is a Scottish biblical scholar who's made her second home in Aotearoa New Zealand. Before she dipped her toes into biblical studies, she gained a degree in psychology and worked as a mental health nurse. Since taking (**very!**) early retirement from academic life in 2021, Caroline has worked as a freelance proofreader and editor. In her spare time, she busies herself with various "passion projects," which usually involve investigating biblical violence in light of contemporary crime narratives, both real and fictional. Her childhood love of crime fiction has never waned, and she's recently turned her hand to writing some murder mysteries of her own.

## Acknowledgments

A massive thanks to Lauren O'Connell for inviting me to write this book and for giving me such invaluable feedback throughout the editing process. It's been a pleasure to get involved in The Bible for Normal People family.

## Behind the Scenes

**Publishing Director** Lauren O'Connell
**Cover Design** Jacqueline Hunt

# Want even more great content?

Head over to **thebiblefornormalpeople.com** where you can find tons of resources to help you explore the Bible.

## CLASSES

Study the Bible's origins, influences, and themes online in your own time.

## BOOKS

Read accessible, engaging Bible commentaries written by scholars just for you.

## PODCASTS

Listen to hundreds of conversations about faith and the Bible.

## COMMUNITY

Join the **Society of Normal People** and get access to:

- All of our classes
- Exclusive Q&As with our team and biblical scholars
- Ad-free podcast stream
- Sneak peeks at upcoming projects
- A thriving online community of people who are curious about the Bible.

For more The Bible for Normal People content, sign up for our newsletter or follow us on socials @thebiblefornormalpeople.